MLA Format

Student Name

Professor Name

Course Name

Date   Title

CULTIVATION I

College Writers Developing the Voice Within, with Readings

GENERAL EDITOR, LAURIE CARTER

—ASSOCIATE EDITORS—

DARYL LYNN DANCE, ELIZABETH CUDDY, LAUREN DELACRUZ, JOYCE JARRETT, CRAIG WYNNE

Kendall Hunt

publishing company

Cover images © Shutterstock.com

Kendall Hunt
publishing company

www.kendallhunt.com

Send all inquiries to:

4050 Westmark Drive

Dubuque, IA 52004-1840

Copyright © 2020 by Kendall Hunt Publishing Company

Text + website ISBN 978-1-7924-1052-9

Text ISBN 978-1-7924-1053-6

Published in the United States of America

Contents

3 College Writing   *43*

5 Structuring and Developing a Paper *83*

5.1 The Introduction *84*

5.2 The Body of the Paper *93*

5.3 The Conclusion *100*

5.4 Structure Across Paper Types *102*

Chapter Summary *104*

6 Personal Writing *107*

6.1 What Is Personal Writing? *108*

Preface

One of the great American novelists and Nobel Prize winner William Faulkner did not have the easiest relationship with writing. In an introduction to *The Sound and the Fury*, he wrote:

> When I began that book, I had no plan at all. I wasn't even writing a book. Previous to it I had written three novels, with progressively decreasing ease and pleasure. . . . The third [book] was shopped about for three years during which I sent it from publisher to publisher with a kind of stubborn and fading hope of at least justifying the paper I had used and the time I had spent writing it. This hope must have died at last, because one day it suddenly seemed as if a door had clapped silently and forever . . . between me and all the publishers' addresses and booklists and I said to myself, Now I can write. Now I can just write. (1973/1994, p. 230)

This is how one of the greatest American novels was born. After Faulkner thought that he no longer had any hope of publication, the ideas that came to him ultimately developed into the great masterwork *The Sound and the Fury*. Similarly, once we move beyond the pressures, doubts, and misgivings that can often plague the start of a writing project, it is possible to find a place where we are able to "just write," and that is when we produce our best work. Writing begins with an idea, and if a writer pursues that idea to its fullest, it can develop into an essay, short story, or a novel. Of course, students taking this course do not have to write a 200-page novel like *The Sound and the Fury*; instead, for college writing, assignments consist of relatively short essays or papers. Whatever the case may be for what a student is writing, all writing begins with an idea that is the start of an exploratory thinking process.

This text offers practical chapters on "College Reading," "College Writing," "Selecting a Topic and Prewriting," and "Structuring and Developing a Paper." Individual chapters on "Personal Writing" and "Exposition" discuss how to identify these types of essay prompts, and how to develop each of these kinds of papers, including the key features unique to each. A chapter on "Revising, Editing, and Proofreading" explains and details the individual steps of the revision process that apply to any paper. This text offers examples of prompts, annotated student papers, and demonstrates fundamental elements of the writing process. A sound understanding of these fundamentals will allow students to gain confidence in their writing process and to ultimately become successful college writers.

From *Essentials of College Writing: Contemporary Applications, 2/E* by Christine M. Connell and Kathy Sole. © 2013 Bridgepoint Education.

Textbook Features

Essentials of College Writing includes a number of features to help students understand fundamental concepts of critical writing and thinking:

- Sample student papers
- Writing in Action exercises
- Chapter summaries
- Key terms
- Sample writing questions
- Sample essay prompts
- Diagrams and visuals

Introduction to College Writing

1

Rido/Shutterstock.com

Learning Objectives

After reading this chapter, you should be able to do the following:

1. Recognize the common misconceptions and fears about the writing process.

2. Describe the challenges and rewards of the writing process.

3. Summarize the difference between formal and informal language, and understand code switching.

4. Explain how to utilize useful tools for writers, including style guides, thesauruses, and etymological dictionaries.

5. Apply the use of resources such as online libraries, writing centers, and tutoring services.

I love that moment at the end of the day, or the end of the week, or the end of the manuscript, which might be a couple of years, when I am reading it over and thinking, "This is what I meant to do. This is how I wanted it to sound."

–Anna Quindlen

From *Essentials of College Writing: Contemporary Applications, 2/E* by Christine M. Connell and Kathy Sole. © 2013 Bridgepoint Education.

Writing can be an enjoyable and rewarding process, and this class is an opportunity for you to strengthen your writing skills and to learn the methods of college writing. The writing process gives back to you, the writer, what you put into it. Writing helps you discover what you think. Have you ever written down your thoughts about a subject in a journal or notebook? If so, chances are that in doing so you learned something about your own thought process. While much of the writing that you will do for a college course will not be personal, all writing is reflective. In fact, journaling your thoughts on any writing assignment can be a great way to start sorting out what you will write in the essay.

One of America's most famous authors, William Faulkner, once claimed that "A writer needs three things: experience, observation, and imagination, any two of which, at times any one of which, can supply the lack of the others" (Faulkner, 1968, p. 248). If Faulkner—who wrote and revised tirelessly—had faith that the writing process could be cultivated so easily, then becoming an effective writer is a possibility for most people. This chapter is an introduction to the tasks, requirements, and elements of writing, and to the resources available to help you create well-written college papers.

1.1 Good Writers Are Made, Not Born

Some students believe that writing is an inborn talent: You either have it, or you do not—but this is completely untrue. So-called "good" writers commit time to working on their writing, including revising. Since writing is an acquired skill, anyone can become a good writer through a combination of hard work and commitment. Reading formal or informal writing extensively is also an excellent way to work on one's writing. Through reading and paying attention to various writing structures and techniques, writers build a stronger vocabulary, a sense of how to organize ideas, and an understanding of writing structure.

You might be surprised to learn that most of the famous authors you have heard of kept to a daily writing schedule of several hours a day and threw away many drafts before arriving at a "final draft." Consider Mark Twain's (1868) description of the writing process: "To get the right word in the right place is a rare achievement. To condense the diffused light of a page of thought into the luminous flash of a single sentence, is worthy to rank as a prize composition just by itself" (para. 3). Good writers practice writing, and the more you write, the more you will see your writing improve. No matter how much or how little natural ability you have, you can develop writing skills and strengthen the skills you currently have. Misconceptions people may have about writing can make them feel disinclined toward the whole subject. Dismissing these misconceptions is perhaps the first step toward becoming a good writer.

Common Misconceptions About Writing

Many people have ideas about writing that are negative and hinder their ability to write well. They may think that writing is, and always will be, difficult for them, or that it is not an important skill to learn, or that it is simply not fun. These misconceptions affect the way many students feel about writing, but luckily, there are several ways to overcome these ideas and create a more enjoyable writing experience.

Myth #1: I'm Not Good at It

Before starting the actual writing process, it is important to first examine your mental attitude about writing. American automobile pioneer Henry Ford is quoted as saying, "Whether you think you can, or you think you can't—you're right." In other words, if you believe you cannot do something, you will probably be unable to do it—not because you do not have the ability, but because you will not devote the time and the energy necessary to develop that skill. Thus, it becomes a self-fulfilling prophecy. An unknown writer once stated this concept succinctly (see *Writing in Action: Watch Your Thoughts*). On the other hand, if you believe you can become a good writer through hard work, and you commit yourself to the writing process, you can certainly improve your writing skills.

Writing in Action: Watch Your Thoughts

Watch your thoughts, for they become words.

Watch your words, for they become actions.

Watch your actions, for they become habits.

Watch your habits, for they become character.

Watch your character, for it becomes your destiny.

—*Unknown*

(San Antonio Light, 1977)

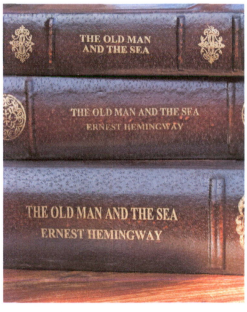

Andrew McDonough/Shutterstock.com

On the difficulty of writing, famous American writer Ernest Hemingway said, "We are all apprentices in a craft where no one ever becomes a master."

Myth #2: Writing Is Easy for Some People but Difficult for Me

Some people seem to write so beautifully. Their writing flows smoothly and is so easy to read that it seems effortless. However, good writers only make it look easy. Do not be fooled; writing is difficult for everyone. Perhaps at some point you had an opportunity to read one of the many books by the celebrated American novelist and short-story writer Ernest Hemingway. Hemingway wrote from the 1920s to 1950s and received two of the most prestigious awards a writer can earn, the Pulitzer Prize in 1953 for his novel *The Old Man and the Sea* and the Nobel Prize for Literature in 1954. Hemingway had a distinctive writing style and generally wrote in simple sentences, using clear, direct words. Often, however, he mixed longer and shorter sentences to add variety and to create drama. This variety of sentence structure can be seen in the opening passage from *The Old Man and the Sea*, shown in *Writing in Action: Opening Passage From* The Old Man and the Sea.

Writing in Action: Opening Passage From *The Old Man and the Sea*

He was an old man who fished alone in a skiff in the Gulf Stream and he had gone eighty-four days now without taking a fish. In the first forty days a boy had been with him. But after forty days without a fish the boy's parents had told him that the old man was now definitely and finally *salao*, which is the worst form of unlucky, and the boy had gone at their orders in another boat which caught three good fish the first week . . . . .

The old man was thin and gaunt with deep wrinkles in the back of his neck. The brown blotches of the benevolent skin cancer the sun brings from its reflection on the tropic sea were on his cheeks. The blotches ran well down the sides of his face and his hands had the deep-creased scars from handling heavy fish on the cords. But none of these scars were fresh. They were as old as erosions in a fishless desert.

Everything about him was old except his eyes and they were the same color as the sea and were cheerful and undefeated.

"Santiago," the boy said to him as they climbed the bank from where the skiff was hauled up. "I could go with you again. We've made some money."

The old man had taught the boy to fish and the boy loved him.

"No," the old man said. "You're with a lucky boat. Stay with them."

"But remember how you went eighty-seven days without fish and then we caught big ones every day for three weeks."

"I remember," the old man said. "I know you did not leave me because you doubted."

"It was papa made me leave. I am a boy and I must obey him."

"I know," the old man said. "It is quite normal."

"He hasn't much faith."

"No," the old man said. "But we have. Haven't we?"

"Yes," the boy said. "Can I offer you a beer on the Terrace and then we'll take the stuff home."

"Why not?" the old man said. "Between fishermen."

The Opening Passage from The Old Man and the Sea *(Hemingway, 1952, pp. 9–11)*

This passage from *The Old Man and the Sea* is an example of Hemingway's deceptively simple style of writing. He was able to convey strong emotions and create vivid visual scenes with his skilled use of language. Hemingway was also meticulous in revising his writing to be as good as he could make it, maintaining that he rewrote the ending of his classic World War I novel, *A Farewell to Arms*, 39 times. Hemingway never described writing as easy. Instead, he said, "We are all apprentices in a craft where no one ever becomes a master." What is the point of practicing something that even the experts agree is difficult? The answer to that question is that writing can become a powerful tool in daily life because we learn something about ourselves in the process, and because it can be rewarding and fun.

Myth #3: Writing Is Not Fun

It is never fun to engage in an activity when you perform poorly, but if you can find an aspect of the prompt or the reading that is interesting to you as your starting point, you will be more interested in the writing process, and will therefore be much more likely to produce good writing. As you become a better writer, you will find that being able to express your thoughts, feelings, ideas, and beliefs clearly and convincingly will give you a sense of enjoyment, accomplishment, and pride. You will also have a tremendous power through which you can share your ideas and influence others. Did you know that becoming a good writer will also help you become a good debater? There have likely been times when you disagreed with someone's political or philosophical interpretation about something, but maybe you were unsure how to express your argument. Becoming a good writer will also allow you to communicate at a higher level verbally.

Myth #4: Writing Is Not Important

Some students believe writing is not important or that they will not need to write in their jobs. Fifty years ago, this belief may have been true, but in our complex and technically oriented society, people in almost every occupation need advanced reading and writing skills. At least one expert believes that the reading and writing skills demanded by many entry-level jobs are even greater than those needed to be successful in college (Daggett, 2002). Almost all jobs today require workers to read highly technical manuals; to write instructions and procedures; and to correspond with customers, management, and even government officials via emails and letters. One business advisory committee estimates that most jobs demand 1½ hours of reading-related tasks every day, such as the ability to read and comprehend safety instructions and signs (Hryciuk, 1995). The idea that you can succeed in the workplace today without good reading and writing skills is a myth. Hopefully, your career goals are in line with your interests, and you work in a field that you enjoy. This means that writing will help you attain your larger goals. In all likelihood, you will also have to write something as part of your job application, which will then be used to assess how qualified you are for a job.

Writing can also be valuable in one's personal life apart from simply securing a job position. Whether you are writing a letter, a blog post, or an email, it is helpful in many arenas of life to be able to communicate clearly and effectively. Regardless of where you are starting from, you can significantly improve in any form of writing you wish to.

Becoming a Good Writer

Writing includes a series of tasks that requires a *set* of skills. The chances are that you already possess certain abilities in some aspects of the writing process, while you may want to strengthen your skills in other areas. Some people have trouble getting started on a writing project; others have no problem generating ideas but have difficulty organizing those ideas. Some writers have storytelling ability, while others seem better at writing informational reports, letters, or instructions. While any sort of natural ability with language is meaningless if an individual does not cultivate that ability, a person who works on cultivating the skills he or she does have can easily exceed the abilities of the so-called "natural born writer."

Master Writing Tasks

One goal of this book is to help you discover your own writing strengths and weaknesses. It is important to consider writing weaknesses so that you can focus on improving in those areas. As you learn the fundamentals of effective writing and sharpen your skills, you will build your writing confidence. You probably will not excel at all writing tasks or at all different types of writing the first time you try them. However, you can make the most of the abilities you have, and you may even discover talents you did not know you possessed. In this course, students may be asked to take diagnostic tests or quizzes. These help assess your writing abilities at the beginning of a term. Your instructors will use these diagnostics to gain insight about the strengths and weaknesses of your writing.

Review the list of writing tasks that are components or steps of a writing assignment in *Writing in Action: Writing Tasks*. Decide which writing tasks you find easiest and which tasks you would like to work on in order to become a stronger writer.

Writing in Action: Writing Tasks

Review this list and place an "S" next to at least three tasks you see as your strengths and a "W" next to at least three tasks that are weaknesses for you. A "strength" does not necessarily mean that you always perform this task well. It just means that you find this task to be one of the easiest aspects of writing, and it does not usually cause you a great deal of trouble. A "weakness" is a task that almost always causes problems for you. In this course, resolve to improve the weak areas you identified.

____ Getting started on a writing assignment

____ Reading and understanding the assignment

____ Finding a topic

____ Generating ideas for your paper

____ Conducting research on the Internet

____ Conducting research using a physical or online library

____ Writing a personal story

____ Writing a paper that explains an issue or shares information

____ Writing a persuasive paper

____ Writing a research paper

____ Creating in-text and reference list source citations

____ Typing the paper on the computer

____ Staying on topic when you write

____ Finding the right words

____ Organizing your ideas

____ Including details and elaborating on your ideas

____ Revising and editing your draft

(continued)

Writing in Action: Writing Tasks *(continued)*

____ Using correct English grammar and punctuation

____ Spelling words correctly

____ Proofreading your work

____ Turning your assignment in on time

This text will teach you (or review for you) the fundamentals of each major writing task. If you have difficulty with a particular writing task, perhaps you have not learned the elements required to perform that task well. If you already know the fundamentals, perhaps you have trouble because you have avoided writing opportunities and have let your skills become dull through disuse. You can think of your writing ability as a muscle: If you do not exercise it, it can become weak from lack of use. On the other hand, as soon as you start practicing again, you will begin to learn and ultimately, to improve.

Practice Writing

As you complete your college degree and expose yourself regularly to written words through your reading and writing, you will naturally strengthen your language abilities and your writing skills. Athletes must train and practice regularly to be at their peak performance level; musicians must practice diligently to maintain the height of their skills. Writers, as well, must write continually to express their ideas with clarity. For this reason, many writing experts suggest keeping a **personal journal** or a diary. Besides being a wonderful way to chronicle your life and to record your experiences, journaling can be a useful tool for both reading comprehension and improving writing skills. Keeping a personal journal gives you an opportunity to think about what you have learned and can help you practice translating your thoughts and feelings into written words. Writing a **blog** (a public or private web journal, usually on a particular subject) on the Internet serves this same purpose; journals, however, are often kept private while blogs are often, but not always, shared with others. (*Tip*: Search the Internet using the keywords "journaling" or "blogging" for more information about these topics or to find journal and blog ideas.) Journaling or blogging may be the way you start to build a positive relationship with writing—and one thing all good writers have in common is that they come to enjoy the writing process.

If you have any fears about writing, you are not alone. Most writers, including some highly successful authors, feel the same way. American writer Natalie Goldberg believes that when we write, "we have to look at our own inertia, insecurities, self-hate, fear that, in truth, we have nothing valuable to say. . . ." (Goldberg, 2005). You may worry that you are not good enough or that no one will like what you have written. Perhaps you are afraid that you will not be able to finish the paper or that you will not be able to start. Or, you may dread exposing your true feelings, hate the frustration you experience when you write, or be concerned about being criticized. Keep in mind that this is a *fear*, but it is not the *truth*. The truth is that we all have valuable insights we can offer on a subject.

However, even with this in mind, it can still be difficult to overcome the fear associated with writing. What is the cure? Self-help guru Susan Jeffers's answer, and title of one of her best-selling books, is *Feel the Fear . . . And Do It Anyway* (2006). In other words, acknowledge the fear or the anxiety. It is natural to be apprehensive or even fearful about putting your ideas on paper, but do not let that fear stop you. As Jeffers explains, doing what we fear builds our confidence in ourselves, and that growing confidence helps make fear disappear. Usually with writing, most of the fear occurs *before* we have begun to write. Once you can move past that and put your first sentence down on the page, most of the feelings of fear will dissolve. It can be useful to remind yourself that what you first write does not have to be perfect. No one's writing is perfect on the first draft, not even the material produced by professional writers! You may want to try to write out your thoughts on a particular subject first without worrying too much about grammar, and then later reread what you have written, trying to make sure your sentences are clear, grammatically correct, and logical. It is important to remember that your sentences do not have to be perfect the moment they are first typed; save time to revise your ideas so that you can smooth out your sentences as much as possible.

Finally, each person approaches writing in a different way. What is most important is that you find a method that works best for you. You may want to start writing by simply brainstorming ideas on a piece of paper; you may want to begin by writing an outline, or plan, of what you intend to say; or, you may simply feel most comfortable by starting with paragraph one. Whatever your method may be, it is useful to try other methods in order to learn what works best for you. It will also help build confidence in your writing skills to gain a deeper understanding of the basic elements of writing, and these elements will be discussed in the next section.

1.2 Common Elements in All Writing

Regardless of the type of document—whether it is a novel, a school paper, a business report, or a speech—all writing is similar in several important ways. The writing situation and its context are always crucial to consider when writing.

The Writing Situation and Context

Whenever you write, you do so for a purpose. You usually have a goal in mind that you are trying to achieve, and that purpose or goal might fall into one of the following categories:

- To tell a story or to share personal opinions or experiences
- To inform, explain, explore, analyze, or interpret ideas
- To convince readers to share your point of view about a subject or to take some action you recommend
- To honor or commemorate someone or something
- To acquire knowledge and/or to organize, analyze, and synthesize information
- To entertain the reader and provide an escape from daily activities

For any writing task, ask questions about the audience for whom you are writing. Are you writing for your college instructor, a friend, your boss, or a customer? How you visualize your anticipated audience affects what and how you write. Just as you would use different language when you talk to your friend than you would if you were talking to your instructor, you want to craft your language to suit your audience when you write.

The Writing Situation

The **writing situation** includes the occasion, audience, the writer's persona or **voice**, and the argument of the writing. The writing situation also determines the **genre** or the type of writing required. For example, if your instructor asked you to give an oral presentation in class, you would not write and memorize an essay. Instead, you would write a presentation outline that would probably include a thesis statement as well as examples to support your main points.

Rawpixel.com/Shutterstock.com

Developing a unique voice, or style of writing, is what differentiates a writer from others. We must also consider the audience when choosing our voice.

You can think of the **occasion** as the reason why you are writing. For instance, if you are writing a eulogy, a speech celebrating the life of a deceased person, the occasion is the funeral ceremony. In this example, the **audience** will include many family members and friends who are there to honor and celebrate the life of the deceased. The audience should be kept in mind while you write; the audience members likely would not appreciate negative comments about the deceased. However, they probably would enjoy positive statements about the person's accomplishments, an overall serious voice, and perhaps even a few respectful jokes about funny things that the deceased did during his or her lifetime. Another aspect of the writing situation is the writer's or speaker's **persona**, or voice, which in the case of a eulogy will likely be somber and express familiarity with the deceased. Finally, part of the writing situation is the **argument** that you are making. In the case of a eulogy, this would likely be a claim about the deceased's greatest qualities. Figure 1.1 illustrates the elements of the writing situation and can be a guide for determining what to write and how to write it.

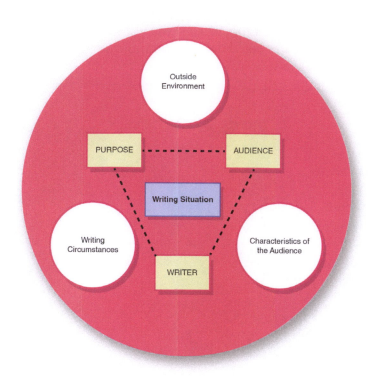

Figure 1.1: The context for writing

Considering elements of the writing situation such as the audience, the purpose for writing, and the outside environment will help you make writing choices that are appropriate for the occasion.

When you are writing for a class, the assignment itself is often the "occasion" for writing. Your "audience" will generally be your instructor or TA. The "persona" or voice in which you write will be your own, but likely with a more formal or academic tone than you would use for writing an email to a friend. And your instructor will often give you an essay prompt from which you will derive an argument. An argument is not a statement of fact; it is an interpretation that can be disagreed with. If a sentence is simply a truth of the text, then it is not yet an argument—add an interpretation about the significance of those details in order to turn the idea into an argument. For example, to say "In *The Great Gatsby*, Jay Gatsby is extremely wealthy" is probably not a sufficient argument on which to write a paper. However, "In *The Great Gatsby*, F. Scott Fitzgerald uses the extreme wealth of Jay Gatsby to demonstrate the corrupting power of money" would be a worthwhile argument to write about because it is a statement that someone could argue against.

As stated above, usually the writing prompt in itself determines your audience, persona, and the occasion. For an additional example, if the assignment asked you to write a speech to be delivered to your class, then that is the occasion. In this case, the audience would refer to your classmates, an educated group of individuals, and of course your instructor. When writing your speech, you should take into consideration the fact that your audience is knowledgeable about the subject and use appropriate formal language. If the speech requires you to take a position on a current topic, a mixture of enthusiasm and seriousness would create a persona or voice that seems reliable. The argument that you would make would be an answer to the essay assignment—for example, arguing that a character in a novel makes a good choice even though it leads to bad results.

You have your own voice, a characteristic style of writing that will be different from the writing of anyone else. These elements of occasion, audience, argument, and persona create a unique writing situation.

Considering Context

In addition to the writing situation, the writing circumstances, outside environment, and characteristics of the audience all play a role in writing. Always consider how the written material will be used. For example, the writing might be read aloud, used only for a classroom assignment, or be published somewhere. If the material is intended to be read orally, this circumstance would change the language and sentence structure of what you write. If your manuscript will be published, the publisher might have some specific language requirements.

The outside environment should also affect your writing, so you might want to think about what is going on in the reader's experience that could influence what you say and how you say it. You might have written about terrorism differently, for example, if you wrote before September 11, 2001, or immediately after the 9/11 attacks.

You will also want to consider the backgrounds and attitudes of the audience. Some questions you could ask yourself about your readers might be:

- How is the audience likely to react to what I have to say?
- Will my readers like or dislike what I have written?
- How important will this topic be to my readers, and what else might they have read about the topic?
- What do readers need to know about this subject?
- How much do they already know?
- What do I want them to think or to know when they have finished reading?

All the factors mentioned above—the occasion, audience, persona, argument, writing circumstances, and outside environment—shape the way in which you will write. Understanding these aspects of the writing situation and context helps you make decisions about such writing issues as the following:

- What type of paper should I write?
- Who is the audience for the paper?
- What point of view should I use—should the writing be in first person (*I*), second person (*you*), or third person (*they* or *the researcher*)?
- Should my language be formal or informal?
- What terms should be defined, and what terms would the audience already know?
- What information should be included, and what should be left out?

Try to keep the elements of the writing situation and context in mind as you write.

We will revisit these issues throughout this course and discuss how to apply them to your college writing assignments. In many cases, instructors will supply the necessary information on the writing situation for your assignment.

Rhetoric

For writing to be effective, to accomplish its purpose, the language must be appropriate. This means that you must make conscious choices about the words you use and the way you use them. When thinking about the rhetorical context for your writing situation, it is crucial to think about rhetorical devices and how you may be using them. The word **rhetoric** refers to the skill of using language effectively and persuasively. Rhetoric first arose as a major field of study under the ancient Greeks, and Aristotle defined it as "the faculty of observing in any given case the available means of persuasion" (Aristotle, 350 BCE). Aristotle described three basic forms of rhetoric or of appealing to the reader. These three forms—pathos, ethos, and logos—will be discussed below.

Appeals to the Reader

When a writer or speaker makes a special appeal to the audience's emotions in order to persuade them, the writer is said to be appealing to the readers' **pathos**. Appeals to pathos are used in public service announcements, advertising, and politics, to name just a few. Examples of such a kind of appeal are the television commercials from the ASPCA, the American Society for the Prevention of Cruelty to Animals. The commercials make an appeal to pathos by making you feel deeply saddened by the examples of animal cruelty that flash across your screen. And that appeal may in fact prompt you to act and donate money or time toward stopping animal cruelty. An appeal to pathos is not always wrong—clearly, animal abuse is a serious ethical issue. But the creators of the commercials did use appeals to pathos in order to persuade you to act. An appeal to **ethos** occurs when speakers emphasize their own credibility and authority on a subject. If someone seems to be an expert on a subject, the chances are that you are more likely to believe what that person is saying. But beware—some people may simply claim they are experts on a topic, and may not actually be. On the other hand, if someone refers to his or her credentials, such as having a Ph.D. on a subject, then that person probably truly is an expert in that area of study. Writers and speakers also sometimes make an appeal to **logos**, or an appeal to the audience's sense of reason and logic. If a writer makes a step-by-step series of claims that add up to a conclusion, that is an appeal to logos. Table 1.1 breaks down the characteristics of these three types of appeals, and provides examples of each.

Table 1.1: Appeals to the reader

pathos	An appeal to the audience's emotions.	Example: How could you live with yourself if you don't donate to this animal shelter? These poor animals need you.
ethos	An appeal to one's credibility or authority on the subject discussed.	Example: I have researched this subject for a very long time, so my interpretation is likely correct.
logos	An appeal to the audience's reason.	Example: Considering these clear statistics, it is only reasonable to conclude that global warming is a real phenomenon.

Persuasion

It is generally assumed that if one sounds logical and reasonable, then one can persuade others. But sometimes an argument may *sound* logical when in fact it is not, so read carefully. At other times the argument may really be logical and the evidence used to support the argument may also be reasonable. Yet the evidence must be more than simply reasonable—the evidence must actually prove what the writer is trying to argue in order for it to be a fair appeal to logos. For instance, a writer can give you statistics that are true, but if they are about an unrelated subject, they really do not prove the writer's argument. If a writer were to give you facts about how the use of toothpaste is clinically proven to reduce cavities, that evidence does not prove that a particular brand of toothpaste is the *best* one at preventing tooth decay. Almost all writing requires you to think critically about the subject you are writing on; always be sure to question evidence, claims, and conclusions a writer makes and make sure they are reasonable and logical.

Formal Versus Informal Language and the Standard College Essay

Informal language tends to be used outside of the classroom and is defined as language you would use when speaking or writing to acquaintances or friends. Our communication may include slang, incomplete sentences, improper capitalization (or no capitalization at all), incorrect grammar, contractions such as "can't" or "don't," or informal language such as the terms "ain't" or "my bad." The writing you do in your college classes should avoid the informal language used when talking, chatting, texting, or emailing with friends. The use of the first-person "I" is usually considered informal language. For the most part, unless you are writing a reflective paper or personal response, using "I" in your writing is unnecessary because it is already clear that the arguments and thoughts on the page are *yours*.

Formal language is more careful than everyday speech, usually sounds serious, is grammatically correct, and avoids slang or other informal language that you would use with friends. It is the standard and most appropriate language for academic and professional papers, legal documents, and business writing. Editors frequently use such language when writing introductions to novels that give insight about the novel's main concerns and themes. For example, in the introduction to Charlotte Brontë's *Jane Eyre*, Michael Mason uses formal language: "*Jane Eyre* is a *thinking* novel, right down to the fine grain of its expression. There is nothing automatic, everything is fresh and considered, to the point where the vocabulary can even teeter on the edge of the outlandish" (Mason, 1996, xiii). Vocabulary, sentence structure, and a tone appropriate for an educated audience are used here.

Formal language is not necessarily pompous or stuffy, nor is it wordy or difficult to read. Formal language is written for an educated audience, including your peers and instructors. It attempts to be clear, accurate, and objective. Your college papers should also contain complete sentences that are organized into logical paragraphs, and you must remember to capitalize properly and check your grammar and punctuation before submitting your assignments. (Do not rely on your word processor's spelling- and grammar-checking programs.) Most forms of college writing require you to write: (1) a thesis statement that is an answer to the essay prompt, (2) body paragraphs with argumentative topic sentences that state what you are going to prove in that paragraph, (3) claims using evidence in your body paragraphs to support your argument, and (4) a conclusion. See the Thesis Development Tool and sample outline in the Writing Center for an example of how all of these pieces can fit together in a typical paper outline.

Formal and Informal Writing and the Personal Essay

The one major exception to the rule about the use of formal language is with the **personal essay**—such an essay asks you to discuss your thoughts on a subject while using the first-person narrative style, and, in some cases, you might use other elements of informal language, depending on the essay prompt and your instructor's requirements.

Personal writing takes many forms, and may not *always* have a thesis or argumentative topic sentences. However, in personal essays written in a college setting, a thesis statement and reasoned argument are likely to be required. In "Mother Tongue," Amy Tan discusses the American stereotype that Chinese Americans cannot excel at the English language:

> Fortunately, I happen to be rebellious in nature and enjoy the challenge of disproving assumptions made about me. I became an English major my first year in college, after being enrolled as pre-med. I started writing nonfiction as a freelancer the week after I was told by my former boss that writing was my worst skill and I should hone my talents toward account management. (Tan, 1990/2007, p. 422).

The use of the first person in this excerpt gives the reader a direct account of the narrator's thoughts and perspective. It is intimate and direct, and gives the reader insight into Tan's desire to counter assumptions made about her based on race. The first-person style may draw us into the narrative more fully and may also enable us to identify with, or relate to, the narrator. Tan invites us to consider some of the negative effects of stereotyping, in this case stereotypes based on race.

Code Switching

Written or spoken language can be thought of as a type of code. If people know the code, they can easily communicate. However, if they do not, communication is extremely difficult. Without being conscious of it, people often change their language to fit the situation or to adapt to the audience. Adapting to the audience is known as **code switching**. Writers should try to gauge their audiences and adapt their language so that the code is something the audience readily understands—otherwise, a writer should not use code at that moment. For example, you may be having a casual conversation with a close friend at work in which you are using slang words such as *dude* or abbreviations such as BFF (best friends forever). If your supervisor or manager approaches and joins the conversation, you might switch codes, lose the slang and any expletives (swear words), and use more formal speech than you were using with your friend.

In certain situations, writers may also use specialized terms, abbreviations, and acronyms at work that people outside one's organization might not understand. In the military, for example, abbreviations such as DoD (Department of Defense) and BOQ (bachelor officers' quarters) are clearly understood by other military personnel. As long as everyone knows the **jargon**, or highly specialized language, it can be very useful as a communication shortcut. However, if an outsider is present and does not understand the terminology, speakers must switch codes to communicate effectively with them. Typically, you would want to avoid using this form of code switching in all formal essay writing. One key to writing a good essay is to define all of your terms.

Code switching also takes place when people who speak more than one language unintentionally use words from different languages when they speak. For example, if you grew up speaking both Spanish and English, you might occasionally use a sentence that contains words from both languages. To make sure your communication is understood in formal essay writing, you must remain conscious of whether you are speaking to someone in Spanish or in English. If, however, you are writing an informal narrative essay, it might be appropriate to use this form of code switching. In "How to Tame a Wild Tongue," Gloria Anzaldúa uses code switching between Chicano Spanish and English, and the effect is striking. She writes: "But Chicano Spanish is a border tongue which developed naturally. Change, *evolución, enriquecimiento de palabras nuevas por invención o adopción* have created variants of Chicano Spanish, *un nuevo lenguaje. Un lenguaje que corresponde a un modo de vivir.* Chicano Spanish is not incorrect, it is a living language" (Anzaldúa, 1987/2007, p. 33). For Anzaldúa, an ever-changing and evolving language corresponds to a way of living. Because Chicano Spanish is an adaptable language, Anzaldúa shows its adaptability by interweaving it with the English language. She is demonstrating what she means by using code switching. In college writing, remember to consciously switch codes from the language of everyday conversation to the formal language of academic papers and the professional workplace. (See *Writing in Action: "Rules" of College Writing*.)

Writing in Action: "Rules" of College Writing

College writing . . .

. . . uses formal language.

. . . is clear, accurate, and uses an objective tone.

. . . avoids jargon, slang, contractions, and the informal language of chatting, texting, or emailing.

. . . uses complete sentences.

. . . organizes sentences into logical paragraphs.

. . . uses proper capitalization, grammar, and punctuation.

1.3 Tools of the Trade

Like any craftsperson, a good writer needs a good set of tools. Some obvious tools for writing in the 21st century are Internet access and a computer with word processing and presentation software. Your school's technology requirements should have been explained to you before you began this class. If you have any questions about these requirements, be sure to contact your college advisor.

General Writing Resources

Ideas for your college writing assignments may come to you when you are not at your computer—when you are traveling, sitting in the dentist's office, cooking dinner, or lying in bed at night. Capture those ideas with your smartphone, tablet, or pen and paper before you forget them.

This text will also be one of the primary tools you will use for this course, along with your course syllabus and, if applicable, a style guide. A **style guide** is a reference that provides additional information to help you improve your writing and brush up on your grammar and punctuation skills. It also contains the essential information and standards you must follow when you write, such as how to format your papers and how to document any outside sources you use. The American Psychological Association (APA) guidelines are the standard for formatting papers and documenting sources in many academic disciplines, and the Writing Center contains resources that explain APA style. Most of your academic papers will conform to the APA-style information found in the Writing Center. You will want to refer to these resources in the Writing Center throughout your degree program as you write your college papers.

Other helpful tools for college writers include a current dictionary (preferably one published within the past 10 years) and a thesaurus, which is an index of words and their synonyms. You might also want to bookmark some of these useful reference websites to help you with your writing:

- www.apastyle.org
  This American Psychological Association website has a tutorial on the basics of APA style, learning resources, an APA style blog, and frequently asked questions and other resources for help with APA format and citations.
- www.onelook.com
  To help you find just the right word, this website allows you to search definitions and synonyms for words in more than 1,000 different dictionaries at the same time. It also contains a reverse dictionary and a "Word of the Day" feature that can help you build your vocabulary. Keep in mind that often synonyms for a word convey a slightly different meaning than the original. Make sure that you understand the word and how to use it before considering using a synonym.
- www.etymonline.com
  This online etymology dictionary gives you the history and origin of words and can help you discover other words that are derived from the same root word.

Writing Resources

Hampton University strives to provide a learning environment that assists you in becoming a successful writer and college graduate. To help you achieve these goals, the university has developed an extensive set of research and writing resources. Be sure to take advantage of these resources, available free of charge, in this class and throughout your degree program. As you begin this course, take the time to familiarize yourself with the resources listed in the sections that follow and make it a habit to refer to them often. They will help you immeasurably in succeeding in not only this course but also in all your college courses and in the workplace.

Library

The Library gives you access, 24 hours a day, 7 days a week, to an extensive collection of library and database resources to help with your college research and writing. In addition, librarians are available to assist you with finding resources for your assignments. Some of the major resources are listed below, and a more detailed list of resources can be found in the library itself. Most of the Library resources have tutorials, advanced search features, tips, and technical support information to help you use them as effectively as possible. Be sure to check these features in each resource. ProQuest and EBSCOhost, the two largest general journal databases, are usually the best place to start your research. Consult Table 1.2 for more information on the databases available to you.

Table 1.2: Research Databases

ProQuest	ProQuest databases provide access to more than 9,800 full-text journals and newspapers, covering all subject areas.
EBSCOhost	EBSCOhost databases include full-text articles from more than 13,000 journals, covering all subject areas.
JSTOR	JSTOR contains academic journals with excellent content in literature, history, and anthropology.
ebrary	ebrary is a collection of over 78,000 electronic books with titles in all disciplines.
CREDO	Credo Reference and World Book are both general reference collections with a wide variety of resources, including encyclopedias, dictionaries.

The library collection is constantly expanding and changing.

Writing Center

Writing support from the Writing Center is another service provided to you. The center provides a wealth of writing resources, some of which are outlined below. If you wish, you can download and print most of these resources to build your own resource library.

- ***Thesis Generator:*** This automated tool can help you develop a clear thesis statement for your academic papers. (We discuss thesis statements in more depth later in this text.) However, you might want to explore this tool now to see how it works. You can use the Thesis Generator as often as you wish to practice developing thesis statements for your academic writing and generating sample outlines. While you should not exclusively rely on the thesis generator, it may be a helpful starting point. If you use the thesis generator, do not simply plug the results into your paper; try to modify the results to make your thesis more complex.

Figure 1.2: Thesis Generator

Thesis Statement Guide Development Tool

Follow the steps below to formulate a thesis statement.

1. State your topic.

> regulating children's television use

2. State your opinion/main idea about this topic.
   This will form the heart of your thesis. An effective statement will

   - express one major idea.
   - name the topic and assert something specific about it.
   - be a more specific statement than the topic statement above.
   - take a stance on an issue about which reasonable people might disagree.
   - state your position on or opinion about the issue.

> parents should regulate the amount of television their children watch

3. Give the strongest reason or assertion that supports your opinion/main idea.

> it is not always intellectually stimulating

4. Give another strong reason or assertion that supports your opinion/main idea.

> it inhibits social interaction

5. Give one more strong reason or assertion that supports your opinion/main idea.

> it shortens children's attention spans

6. Include an opposing viewpoint to your opinion/main idea, if applicable. This should be an argument for the opposing view that you admit has some merit, even if you do not agree with the overall viewpoint.

> television can be educational

7. Provide a possible title for your essay.

> Touch that Dial!

> Submit

- *Writing resources:*
  - Writing samples of some types of college assignments that you will be asked to prepare during your degree program
  - Writing and grammar tutorials, exercises, and handouts to help you improve your writing skills and avoid plagiarism
  - eBook resources such as guidelines and tutorials
  - Microsoft® Office guides to help you improve your use of Microsoft® Word and PowerPoint software
- *Business writing guides:*
  - Samples of case studies, executive summaries, and papers that you will be asked to write in many business courses
  - Grammar handouts
- *APA research guides and samples* to help you: (1) understand and use APA style and (2) develop research papers. This section of the Writing Center also contains RefWorks, a Web-based tool that can assist you in creating a reference page for your college papers.

As we discussed earlier, writing gives us a great power to impact and to influence others. We must always remember to use this power responsibly, which means to be professional when we write, to respect the views of others, to use technology resources in ways that do not violate laws or the rights of others, and to not engage in academic dishonesty. We discuss your responsibilities as an ethical writer in more detail in Chapter 3.

fizkes/Shutterstock.com

Plagiarism is the use of another person's or writer's language, research, or ideas without citing and giving credit to that source of information. Many people may think of plagiarism as simply rewriting someone else's sentences into one's own paper; although this is a clear form of plagiarism, it certainly is only one way to plagiarize. Other forms of plagiarism include:

- Copying text from any printed material that is not your own and placing it into your paper without acknowledging the source
- Altering someone else's text by changing some of the words and not acknowledging it as a paraphrase
- Copying and pasting sentence fragments, whole sentences, or even paragraphs from Internet sources or someone else's writing without citing
- Using any fragment of another student's work or ideas is considered an act of *collusion*. Colluding with another student, even if the student agrees to "share" her writing, is a serious act of academic dishonesty, and is a form of plagiarism.
- Using materials purchased online or elsewhere

- Reusing old papers of your own for a writing assignment without the instructor's permission far in advance of the due date
- Paraphrasing or summarizing another writer's work or thoughts without citing
- Summarizing or using any ideas that are not your own. (In other words, if an idea was not one that you developed on your own and you were introduced to this idea through some other written source, you *must* acknowledge it by citing the work.)

Plagiarism, therefore, is *any attempt* to include *any amount* of someone else's ideas, thoughts, research, language, or even the way the writer has structured his or her ideas *without acknowledging* the fact that another source is being used. However, if some fact is common knowledge, you do not need to cite it. The year a major event occurred is common knowledge. If, for instance, you say that World War II began in 1939, you do not need to cite that information because it is common knowledge. But any interpretation of historical facts, lesser-known information, or original research needs to be cited. As a general rule, if you are in doubt as to whether or not you should cite, then cite. If you are unsure, you should also ask your instructor about the use of sources in your writing. Your writing instructor will be happy to answer these questions since you are trying to be academically honest.

To put it in context, consider the different ways students might incorporate a piece of someone else's writing into their own essay. In Johanna M. Smith's "'Cooped Up': Feminine Domesticity in *Frankenstein*," she indicates that "no women in the novel speak directly: everything we hear from and about them is filtered through the three masculine narrators . . . these women seldom venture far from home, while the narrators and most of the other men engage in quests and various public occupations" (Smith, 1992, p. 270). Here are three examples of ways in which students might use the above quote:

1. Student A: In *Frankenstein*, no women in the novel speak directly: Everything we hear from and about them is filtered through the three masculine narrators. **(This paper is plagiarizing the scholar's article because it uses Smith's language and does not cite it.)**
2. Student B: Women do not get to speak in the novel *Frankenstein*. This is because men are in control in the story. Male narrators tell us everything about the women in the novel. The women do not really go far from home. The men, on the other hand, engage in public outings. **(This paper is also plagiarizing because it paraphrases Smith's ideas and does not cite the article.)**
3. Student C: As Johanna M. Smith notes, women are mostly silenced in the novel *Frankenstein* because they do not have their own voice. For the most part, male characters tell readers what the women think. Women stay mostly within the private sphere of the home, whereas men frequently act in the public sphere and also engage in travel (Smith, 1992). **(This paper uses Smith's article in a way that is acceptable. This student rephrases Smith's language in the student's own words and cites the article.)**

As an aid toward promoting academic honesty, some classes use the online research tool Turnitin (*www.turnitin.com*). Your paper is uploaded to the website, and then Turnitin compares your paper to all other papers in the system and to all content from the Internet, and picks up matches to other materials in the event of plagiarism. With each assignment, your instructor will check Turnitin to evaluate the possibility of plagiarism.

Plagiarism has academic consequences. Plagiarism may result in receiving no credit on the assignment in question, failing the entire course in which the plagiarism was committed, and/or dismissal from the university. Depending on the case, the university reserves the right to carry out other academic consequences. That said, you have absolutely nothing to worry about if you do not plagiarize.

Chapter Summary

This chapter began by discussing some of the concerns and questions many students have about writing. Hopefully the information in this chapter has convinced you that the wide range of resources and tools you have at your school can help you build your writing skills and overcome any anxieties or fear you have about putting your ideas down on paper. As we embark on our studies of college writing, consider adopting the view of writing suggested by Donald M. Murray, who has been dubbed "America's greatest writing teacher" (Newkirk & Miller, 2009). Rather than think of your academic papers as products you must produce, think of writing them as a process of discovery. In Murray's words, writing can be an exciting "process of exploration of what we know and what we feel about what we know through language. It is the process of using language to learn about our world, to evaluate what we learn about our world, to communicate what we learn about our world" (cited in Newkirk & Miller, 2009, p. 2).

To complete the writing tasks you will face in school and in your career, you must develop a set of skills and continually practice to improve those skills. Understanding the writing situation, the context, and language choices is critically important to writing effectively. For your college papers, considering the context should also remind you to switch codes from the informal language of everyday conversation to the more formal language required in college classes and on the job.

The Library, Writing Center, and writing coaches are there to help—but you will only obtain the help you need if you take initiative and ask for it. Students should also keep the plagiarism guidelines in mind; never hesitate to ask a teaching assistant if you are unsure whether or not a method of writing is plagiarism.

Remember, writing is never easy; it is hard work. However, being successful in college and in the workplace requires that you write well. You have all the tools and resources you need to achieve this goal. The rest is up to you. Learning to write well can be one of the most important accomplishments of your life.

Key Terms

argument The position a writer takes on a subject, or an interpretation he or she makes about a text. An argument is not a statement of fact; it is an interpretation that can be disagreed with.

audience The individuals for whom an author is writing or to whom he or she is speaking.

blog An online journal space in which a writer frequently records thoughts, either publicly or privately, on a particular topic.

code switching Alternating languages and/ or style according to what one's audience will understand. Code switching might include the use of informal language, multiple languages, expressions, or acronyms that only certain audiences will understand.

ethos A speaker's or writer's credibility or authority to speak on a particular subject.

formal language The standard and most appropriate language for academic and professional papers, legal documents, and business writing. Formal language usually sounds serious, is grammatically correct, and avoids language that would otherwise be used in more casual settings.

genre The type of writing being used in a given writing situation.

informal language The type of language used when speaking or writing to acquaintances or friends. It may include slang, incomplete sentences, improper capitalization (or no capitalization at all), incorrect grammar, and contractions.

jargon A specialized language particular to a group of people, usually of a particular profession or group. Specialized language can exclude those who do not belong to the group because they may not understand the language or terms being used.

logos An attempt to persuade by using reasoning and logic. This may include using clear examples, facts, or statistics.

occasion The reason for writing, or what someone is writing for.

pathos An attempt to persuade by making appeals to the audience's emotions.

persona The voice used when writing or speaking; a unique character to one's own writing.

personal essay A type of essay that typically uses the first person to convey the thoughts, feelings, experiences, and ideas of the writer. It may or may not take a position at some point in the essay. Most of the topic sentences in a personal essay are not argumentative.

personal journal A place to record ongoing personal experiences. Personal journals can be shared broadly or with no one. It is helpful to keep a personal journal to keep track of ideas for a writing assignment.

plagiarism The use of another person's or writer's language, research, or ideas without citing and giving credit to that source of information. Any ideas or language that derive from someone else's writing must be cited, even when paraphrasing.

rhetoric The use of language in order to persuade an audience. Someone who is trying to be persuasive should carefully consider what will be persuasive for the particular audience while writing.

style guide A reference book that provides information on how to improve writing, grammar, and punctuation. It also contains essential information and standards that must be followed when writing, such as how to format a paper and how to document any outside sources used.

voice The character of the writer or speaker that is conveyed through the material. A writer's voice is synonymous with persona.

writing situation The occasion, audience, writer's voice, and argument of the writing. The writing situation also determines the genre required.

College Reading

Bo1982/Shutterstock.com

Learning Objectives

After reading this chapter, you should be able to do the following:

1. Contrast active with unfocused reading.

2. Describe the four key steps that are essential to success when beginning a new college course.

3. Identify the key strategies to engage in order to actively read a text, including annotation, a reading journal, and brainstorming.

4. Analyze the components of the SQ3R method, or Survey, Question, Read, Recite, and Review.

5. Differentiate the different key words and action verbs, and understand their implications.

Reading is to the mind what exercise is to the body.

—Joseph Addison (ThinkExist, 2010a)

Chapter 1 explored attitudes about writing, identified common elements in all types of writing, and outlined the writing tools and resources available to assist you in these efforts. This chapter offers guidance on how to help you meet the requirements for well-written college papers, including a discussion and demonstration of active reading strategies, and step-by-step strategies for reading different types of course materials. Good college writing begins with effective reading, and college courses generally require a great deal of both. Most people have been reading for so long that it is easy take its importance for granted. Cultivating the skills of active reading is the first step in learning to become a good writer; if you can thoughtfully interpret what you are reading, you have a much greater likelihood of writing material that is appropriately engaged with the text and the assignment.

2.1 Reading to Write and Learn

When you read novels or other fictional writing, you usually do so to escape your daily routine and to relax from other activities. You probably start at the beginning of the book, read every word, and occasionally lose yourself in the story. Because you are reading for escape or for entertainment, it does not matter how quickly or slowly you read. You can read at your own pace and passively follow along with the story. In your college courses, however, you cannot be a passive reader; college reading requires **active reading**, a method that includes reading with a pen in hand and marking up the terms and phrases that seem significant (or using the highlight tool when reading an ebook). When you are an active reader, you are reading for a purpose. You look for main ideas and let the structure of the reading material, such as the headings and subheadings, help you decide what is most important. Active readers are reading to interpret rather than just gain a basic understanding of the content of the text. Active reading enables you to understand what you are reading and equips you with the skills you need to respond to writing assignments, for exams, or for use on the job or in other aspects of your life. Though some may believe that they will not need the content in this chapter for employment purposes, active reading is an invaluable skill that is needed for most careers that require a college degree.

Reading Misconceptions

Perhaps the most common reading misconception is the idea that you can read effectively while multitasking. Using email, online shopping, searching the Web, or checking social media outlets while also trying to read is extremely detrimental to the reading process. Avoid technological distractions of all kinds while you read because they move some of the focus away from your assignment and the texts. Students also very commonly turn on the TV in the "background" while studying, but the problem is that what was meant as "background" noise moves into the "foreground"—in other words, students ultimately end up focusing on what is on TV and become

Ginny Filer/Shutterstock.com

Effective reading requires your full attention, in an environment without technological distractions.

distracted from their reading. Of course, life puts many demands on us, and it may not always be possible to do your reading in an environment where nothing else is going on. However, when possible, give reading your full attention and avoid multitasking.

Reading to Write

There are two important links between reading and writing. One of these is that reading is one of the best ways to improve your writing. Most good writers learn how to write well through reading rather than through memorizing grammar rules. In fact, reading provides better examples of how to use the English language than simply practicing grammar exercises would. The truth is that reading any form of writing on a regular basis helps writers gain an increased knowledge of writing structures, grammar, clarity, and organization. It is not necessary to constantly read novels or academic writing to achieve this benefit; reading popular social and political magazines and short articles will help as well, as long as they are well written. Not only will you gain more out of reading what interests you, but you will also become a stronger writer because you will automatically notice correct grammar usage, a variety of writing styles, and a variety of narrative structures as you read.

The second fundamental link between reading and writing is that one *must* read a text very carefully in order to write well about it. Close reading requires you to notice details, repetitions, metaphors, similes, symbolism, and/or themes and to develop an understanding of how they—or any other literary devices—function in a text. A good method of reading may start by taking note of terms, phrases, or short clauses that stand out to the reader or that seem significant. As you read, highlight, circle, or underline the language that seems most important. When you notice a recurring theme, for instance, take note of it each time it appears in the text, and ultimately try to trace how that theme or concept develops over the course of the reading. Because all great writing begins with careful reading, students should read a text a few times. On the second reading, more connections between ideas and concepts will become apparent. For most college papers, direct citation is required in the body paragraphs, and one must develop an argument or interpretation about the evidence of the text, so it is necessary to pay attention to possible evidence one might use in a paper while reading. The evidence should directly guide a writer's interpretation, not the other way around: One of the biggest mistakes writers sometimes make is coming up with an "answer" to an essay prompt first and then trying desperately to find evidence to support that answer. Writing should work in the reverse—what the text says and what it suggests is the first step in writing a paper, and the text should in turn guide the writer's interpretation and response to the essay prompt. It is artificial to produce an answer to an essay prompt based on opinion rather than on a careful interpretation of what the text is saying.

Reading to Learn

Course materials usually consist of the course guide (or syllabus), assigned text(s) and other readings, and, in online courses, your instructor's guidance, announcements, and the link to your weekly course assignments. A major mistake some students make is that they fail to read some of these materials, often as a result of procrastination. As a result, they miss important information or fail to prepare their written assignments properly, and their grades suffer. Find a relatively quiet place to read, such as a library's reading room, a bench in a park, a quiet room in your home free of distractions, or if some background noise is good for you, then a coffee shop. Whatever the case may be, it is important that you are comfortable where you are reading and that you can concentrate. Begin your reading assignments immediately. If you read a little bit of material each day, you will have a much easier time completing the reading assignment—and, you will probably digest the material better because you read carefully and gave yourself time to process what you read.

To ensure that you have all the information you need to be successful in your courses, follow the four steps below when you begin a college course.

> **Step 1**: Read the course guide or syllabus thoroughly before the course begins. Pay particular attention to any learning outcomes. Learning outcomes or learning objectives reflect knowledge you are expected to gain by the time you complete the course. Keep these learning outcomes or objectives in mind throughout the course. They are clues to the purpose of the reading materials and the course assignments. It is a good idea to read the entire assignment before reading the assigned text. You can read the text with more care if you first know what your writing assignment requires. The writing assignments, then, serve as a guide for how to read and what to look for in a text.

> **Step 2:** Each week, check your course calendar if applicable, and read the week's information in the syllabus, as well as any emails or announcements from your instructor. Begin with the syllabus. The syllabus (or course guide) is likely to explain the goals and topics for the week and provide directions and additional information about the weekly topics and assignments. Announcements will notify the class of any assignment changes and provide other important information and the calendar, if your course has one, is likely to indicate the due dates for all assignments and exams.

> **Step 3**: As soon as possible each course week, complete the text reading, breaking it up into parts, and any other assigned reading materials. Use the SQ3R reading strategy, described later in the chapter, for lengthy reading assignments.

> **Step 4**: Finally, when you have completed your text and other assigned reading, read your discussion and written assignment prompts again carefully. Make sure you clearly understand the purpose of each assignment, the intended audience, the rhetorical context, and the specific assignment requirements. Your instructor will help you understand these elements of the writing situation, but you should definitely ask if you have any questions about the assignment. When you read the assignment for a second time, follow the guidelines in Section 2.2: Strategies for Active Reading.

In addition to these general reading guidelines a student can apply to any class, it is crucial to understand that different types of reading materials in college classes require different reading strategies.

2.2 Strategies for Active Reading

If you learn how to become an effective active reader, you will be impressed with the results. Learning how to become an active reader does take practice, but each time you practice the skills below you will improve in this crucial skill set.

Annotating and Note Taking

Annotating means writing a note—in the margin of the document you are reading or on a separate piece of paper—that explains or comments on what you have read. The notes you write on a text to help you keep track of key ideas are called *annotations*. Be creative and experiment until you find a recording system that works well for you. If you are using an ebook, chances are that you can highlight and annotate electronically. If you have a printed copy of a text including the reading or writing assignment, you should always read with a pen or pencil and highlighters in hand. If you are unsure what a paragraph or sentence suggests, mark it with a question mark. Indicate surprising moments in the text with an exclamation point. Respond to interesting sections of the text by writing down statements, questions, or ideas you have about them. Use different color highlighters for different themes you notice. Perhaps you see that nature and gender are themes in the text—try using one color highlighter for nature and a separate one for gender. This is a method for organizing your annotations. If you are reading a hard copy, you can also use sticky notes to keep track of your main ideas about the text. You do not need to mark everything you read; part of active reading is learning to distinguish between which material is important and which is less important thematically or in terms of content. When you are done reading a text, your annotations act as a series of interactions between yourself and the text you are reading. This dialogue with the text can and should help you organize a paper about that text. Here is an example of how to effectively annotate a passage from Sophocles's *Antigone*, a statement made by King Creon:

fizkes/Shutterstock.com

Taking notes directly on your text is called *annotating*. This practice can help you remember key concepts and record your reactions to interesting passages.

27

> Sons are more important for kings

That's what a man prays for: to produce good sons—/a household full of them, dutiful and attentive,/so they can pay his enemy back with interest/and match the respect their father shows his friend./But the man who rears a brood of useless children,/what has he brought into the world, I ask you?/Nothing but trouble for himself, and mockery/from his enemies laughing in his face. (Sophocles, 1984, pp. 715–722).

> Sons should fight the enemy

Reflection: *According to this passage, the role of sons is very important to fathers, and maybe especially to kings, since King Creon is speaking. Sons are necessary for warfare—they are needed to fight the "enemy." "Useless children" seem to be those who refuse to fight in warfare, and maybe daughters are also considered part of that category.*

You may have started the passage by wondering what kind of statement would be made about the value of sons, and you may have been surprised to read that King Creon sees sons as necessary for warfare. By the end of the excerpt, it seems that King Creon is making a clear statement that any son who would not go to war for him would be an embarrassment. It seems, then, that perhaps politics matter more to King Creon than his family. It is crucial that when you are reading a text you are doing your best to create an honest interpretation of the text that is well supported by what the text says. Avoid immediately disagreeing with a text or assuming it is uninteresting because these approaches will make you incapable of understanding the text. You might ask yourself: "Would the author consider this to be a fair interpretation of the text?" If the answer seems to be no, then reread portions of the text where you may have become stuck and try to develop a more accurate reading.

As you read, remember to keep the learning outcomes in mind and to continually ask yourself, "Does this information answer the heading question?" and "Is this information I need to know?" If the answers to these questions are yes, read the material carefully and record it in some way. You should always read with a purpose, whether it is to answer questions your instructor has asked you about a text, to answer your own questions about the text, or to organize your thoughts for a paper.

Journaling and Reflection

If, while you are reading, you identify certain pages that seem important, you might want to write down the page numbers in a **reading journal**, which is a place where writers record their initial thoughts and impressions of a text, and may later brainstorm ideas and outline possible main points for the draft of an essay. Writers should especially note the elements of a text that are most interesting or that stand out in some way—there are reasons why certain pieces of text stand out. An informal journal will probably help you think about and ask questions in class about the text. The more engagement you have with the text, the stronger your understanding will be. After noting key phrases and terms, writers reflect on those terms to think about their significance. Reflection leads to brainstorming potential ideas that a writer might use in a paper. **Brainstorming** is a necessary step that allows you to synthesize the material and what you are learning from it.

Survey, Question, Read, Recite, and Review

Ideally, writers use a variety of strategies when approaching texts. Another method of approaching a text is the **SQ3R method**, (see *Writing in Action: SQ3R Method*), an abbreviation which stands for Survey, Question, Read, Recite, and Review (Huber, 2004). SQ3R is a useful strategy for reading books and other lengthy reading materials. This strategy is simple to follow, and it can improve your understanding of what you read.

Writing in Action: SQ3R Method

SQ3R =

1. Survey (skim headings, subheadings, chapter summary, charts, and tables in text).
2. Question (turn headings and subheadings into questions).
3. Read (read to find the answers to your questions and record the answers by highlighting, underlining, or taking notes).
4. Recite (summarize what you learned by telling someone else or writing it down).
5. Review (go back and read your notes or information that you highlighted or underlined to reinforce learning and to commit the information to memory).

Survey

The term *survey* means to preview information. Before reading a chapter, skim or flip through it and read the bold headings that divide the text into different sections. These headings are an outline of the chapter. They will show you how the chapter is organized and give you the main ideas the chapter will cover. As you survey the chapter, also pay attention to any hints, tips, or other material shown in the margins or in hyperlinks. This information is formatted to make it stand out from the rest of the text, and it usually summarizes major points or provides helpful information. If you are doing research, or are simply interested in learning more about a topic, look at the text's index and bibliography. An **index** can include a list of authors and concepts referred to in the text. If you want to see how many references a text makes to Darwin, flip to the index and see if there is an entry. If there is no entry, the text likely is not relevant to your studies. Bibliographies are equally useful resources for readers and researchers. If a text is useful to you and you want to read more texts that relate to the subject matter, the **bibliography** (or reference list) tells you what research the author of the text you are reading relied on. If a text refers to another author whose approach seems particularly interesting, you can turn to the bibliography and then locate these texts.

Next, examine all graphs, pictures, diagrams, and tables. They also summarize information in a clear and concise way. (Remember the old saying, "A picture is worth a thousand words.") Finally, read the introductory and summary paragraphs at the beginning and end of the chapter. These paragraphs point out what to look for in the chapter and recap the most important information.

Question

After your chapter survey, go back to the beginning of the chapter and start reading. As you come to each of the chapter headings or subheadings, change it to a question (using the words *who*, *what*, *where*, *when*, *why*, or *how*). Then try to answer the question as you read. For example, this chapter's heading or title is "College Reading." Change this heading to a question: "What is college reading?" As you read, try to find information in the chapter that answers that question. Do the same for the chapter headings and subheadings. The first heading is "Reading to Write and Learn." Change this heading to a question such as "What does reading actually have to do with writing?" As you read this section of the text, look for information that answers your question. The first subheading under "Reading to Write and Learn" is "Reading Misconceptions." Again, change this heading to a question: "What are reading misconceptions, and why are they important?" Yet another question to consider is: "Do I actually believe in some of these misconceptions?" Looking for answers to these questions means that you are engaging the text, and creating your own dialog with it.

There is no right or wrong way to form the question. Just follow this questioning method with each chapter heading and subheading as you come to it in your reading: First form a question and then read the section to answer the question. Challenging yourself in this way will help you maintain interest in what you are reading and improve your understanding of the text.

Read

Think about what you are reading and what it means. Because you are reading for information that you may need to retrieve later for an exam or a written assignment, develop a system to record important information as you read it. You might want to underline or highlight the information that answers your question or that you think is important. Or, you can use an asterisk (*), an exclamation point (!), or a question mark (?) to mark passages you think are particularly important to remember. You should always feel ready to write notes in the margins about important information as you read. Some students take notes in a notebook and then use different colored marking pens to circle or highlight specific information. If you are reading electronically, then add comments electronically or on a separate sheet of paper. Try to annotate as you read regardless of what you are reading.

Recite

After you have finished reading a section of the book or other lengthy reading material, make sure you understand what you have read by trying to restate it in some way. Reciting does not necessarily mean you have to say it out loud. You can recite what you learned to yourself aloud (or silently) if you wish, but you might also tell someone else what you learned, discuss it in a written discussion post, or write a short paragraph in a notebook that summarizes what you read. However you choose to "recite," it is important that you recap what you learned in some way. You might want to go back to the question you formed from each section heading and, in your own words, answer the question; even better, write down the answer. The answers to the section questions will help you study for future exams. You may even recite material to yourself while you are getting ready in the morning or cooking dinner. You may not have all of your questions about a text answered while you are sitting in front of it. Likely you will need to reflect afterwards and this will contribute to your larger reading of the text.

Think of reciting as a type of self-test to make sure you clearly understand what you read and to reinforce the material in your mind. If you do not clearly understand it, go back and read it again or ask your instructor or other students to help you clarify the meaning.

Review

Finally, review the most important information by going back and looking over the underlined, marked, or highlighted information or by rereading or typing your handwritten notes. Imagine the sort of quiz questions you might be asked on the material and make sure you have the information to answer those questions. When you are finished reading the assigned text, reread what you have written and try to summarize the main points or ideas you think the text is pointing you toward. Try to summarize in order to gain a sense of what you think is valuable in the text.

Reading Visuals

Learning how to read visuals is an art form itself. Your readings may also include simple visuals such as tables, illustrations, or graphics to make information more understandable. Whenever students encounter visuals in their reading assignments, they should always pause and take time to consider what the visual is telling them and how it assists them in their understanding of the course material. Images in reading may help you if you are more of a visual learner. Refer back to tables, graphs, and charts that seem to simplify information and clarify ideas that seemed otherwise unclear as you read.

2.3 Reading for Academic Success

How can you apply reading methods to discussion questions and written assignments for college? The primary methods for understanding assignments consist of learning how to read for key words and action verbs. When taken together, key words and action verbs indicate the concepts the essay must attend to.

Reading for Key Words and Action Verbs

When you read your assignments, create a list of key words and phrases—important nouns, verbs, adjectives, or adverbs that describe or explain the assignment requirements (see Figure 2.1 and Table 2.1). Refer to these key words and phrases often while you are writing your discussion posts and your written assignments to make sure you do not veer off track. In 1956, a group of researchers headed by psychologist Benjamin Bloom developed a taxonomy, or classification system, for educational objectives. Known as Bloom's Taxonomy, this classification system uses specific action verbs to help you understand what you are being asked to do in an assignment and how you will be graded (cited in Halawi, Pires, & McCarthy, 2009).

Undrey/Shutterstock.com

Paying close attention to action verbs in course documents will help you understand assignments and ensure your final submission is relevant and thorough.

Figure 2.1: Anderson's revised version of Bloom's Taxonomy

Bloom's Taxonomy posits a hierarchy of learning skills, in which lower-level skills are preconditions for higher-level skills. A student of Bloom's, Louis Anderson, revised the taxonomy in 2000, using action verbs to emphasize the thinkers' cognitive processes.

Adapted from: Anderson, L. W. and David R. Krathwohl, D. R., et al (Eds..) (2001). A taxonomy for learning, teaching, and assessing: A revision of Bloom's taxonomy of educational objectives. *Boston, MA: Allyn & Bacon. pp. 67–68.*

Table 2.1: Defining terms from Anderson's revision of Bloom's Taxonomy

Creating	Directly creating a unique interpretation of the text that is a result of the learner's individual thought processes and selections about which pieces of text are significant and why.
Evaluating	Evaluating the effect of the selected details by developing the meaning of the language.
Analyzing	Analyzing these selected details to discuss their significance.
Applying	Applying your understanding and memory of details by selecting and transferring these details onto a sheet of paper.
Understanding	Understanding that these concepts may be linked with one another and may suggest significance.
Remembering	Remembering key details, phrases, and terms that connect with one another.

The learning outcomes for your college courses and for your course assignments will likely use specific verbs that explain what the assignment calls for. Refer to Table 2.2 each time you receive an assignment. After you have identified the key words and phrases in the assignment, locate the action verbs in this table, underline them, and then list them. Then read the columns "Objective" and "Assignment Requirements" for that verb to determine what is expected of you. When you read your discussion and written assignments, create a list of all key words and phrases. Assignments require a student's interpretation of action verbs, objectives, and assignment requirements. Table 2.2 describes what certain verbs mean and what they require of you in an assignment.

Table 2.2: Action verbs

Action Verbs	Objective	Assignment Requirements
Define	Show that you understand.	State the meaning of a term.
Identify, label, list, memorize, name, order, quote, recall, recognize, repeat, reproduce, select, state, tell	Show that you remember what you have learned.	Demonstrate your knowledge or recall of information, dates, events, places, or major theories.
Associate, categorize, classify, demonstrate, describe, differentiate, discuss, distinguish, estimate, explain, express, extend, group, indicate, interpret, paraphrase, predict, review, show, sort	Show that you understand.	Interpret facts, restate information in your own words, or demonstrate that you comprehend or grasp the meaning of information or how ideas are connected. Give reasons why or explain how something happened.
Apply, calculate, change, complete, discover, experiment, extrapolate, illustrate, manipulate, modify, operate, practice, relate, solve, test, translate, use	Apply what you have learned or show how something works.	Solve problems or put a theory into practice using information you have learned or show how you can use the information, methods, concepts, or theories in a new situation or a practical manner.
Analyze, arrange, connect, deduce, distinguish, divide, examine, infer, interpret, order, organize, select, test	Analyze ideas or determine how the parts relate to the whole, how something works, what it means, or why it is important.	Break something into parts to show that you can isolate components or important information or recognize patterns, hidden meanings, relationships, or the internal structure of something.
Arrange, assemble, build, combine, compose, construct, create, design, develop, devise, formulate, generalize, hypothesize, integrate, invent, modify, plan, predict, prepare, rearrange, report, substitute	Synthesize, or put ideas together.	Combine parts into a whole, predict or draw conclusions from given facts, blend knowledge from different areas to show how it is related, or combine old ideas and use them in a new way.
Assess, choose, compare, conclude, contrast, convince, criticize, decide, defend, define, discriminate, estimate, evaluate, grade, investigate, judge, justify, measure, rank, recommend, support	Evaluate, or judge, ideas.	Assess or judge the value of something, make logical choices and support those choices, or show how items are similar or different.
Summarize	Show understanding by concisely retelling facts and ideas.	List the main points.

Source: Adapted from Bloom, 1956.

Understanding Discussion Questions and Written Assignments

The SQ3R strategy works well for reading and understanding lengthy articles. However, when you read your discussion assignments and written assignments, you must use a different strategy and read more closely, focusing on recurring concepts, themes, and problems that appear in the text. In fact, it is usually a good idea to reread the text you have been assigned at least once, so that you can trace details, concepts, and themes you may have missed the first time you read. Did you know that your instructors likely reread the text you have been assigned every single time they teach it? This is because active reading makes details clear; a second reading of a text also allows you to make many more connections than you noticed the first time you read. Discussion and writing assignments have specific requirements that also need to be read carefully. Often, students lose points on their discussion posts and college papers because they do not answer all the questions asked in the assignment or they fail to address all the elements the assignment requires.

Discussion Questions and Posts

If your course requires discussion posts, there are likely specific guidelines that you should familiarize yourself with. If you have questions about these guidelines, please do not hesitate to ask your instructor for clarification. Some possible guidelines may include:

- Read the discussion board requirements and your instructor's guidance thoroughly to make sure you understand the discussion assignment.
- Make certain your posting answers all questions and addresses all issues required in the discussion assignment.
- Your initial post should contribute to the topic. It should demonstrate that you have read, understood, and critically evaluated the topic. Give examples and cite specific sentences or paragraphs from the text or from outside research to support your statements.
- Relate the topic to your own experiences. Consider using examples from your personal experiences and discuss how they relate to the topic under discussion.
- Review grammar, punctuation, and spelling and proofread your posts before submitting them.

Like your written papers, your discussion posts are likely to be graded in part on the content, completeness, and quality of your writing. Your posts do not have to include a title page, but they do need to be written in complete sentences. Unless otherwise instructed, you must include a reference for all outside sources you use in your posts. Because discussion posts mimic the types of discussions held in college classrooms, they can typically be written in a formal conversational tone. However, the language must be appropriate for formal college writing. In other words, avoid slang expressions, abbreviations, and the informal language of personal emails or text messages, and always check your posts for spelling, grammar, and punctuation before you submit them. Posts should directly respond to questions your instructor is asking or directly engage with the text and contribute something meaningful to the class discussion. Writing brief responses such as "I disagree," or "I completely agree" are not sufficient responses. If you only discuss your personal opinion and do not give evidence from the text, this will likely result in a poor discussion post, unless your instructor specifically says no citation is necessary. In discussion posts, you must always include reference information for any outside sources that you consulted. All ideas that are not your own must have references. One discussion post assignment asks students to reflect on the conclusion of Joyce Carol Oates's short story "Where Are You Going, Where Have You Been?" (Oates, 1966). In this short story, Arnold Friend, a virtual stranger to the story's protagonist, Connie, demands that she gets into his car, or he will harm her family. The reader is left with the uncertainty of knowing what exactly happens to Connie or why she felt compelled to listen to him. Here is an academically appropriate response for a classroom audience on this ambiguous conclusion:

> Though many people can read the same piece of poetry or prose, each of us gains a different perspective of the piece because of our life circumstances. One example of this can be found with my interpretation of the essay in our text titled "Where Are You Going, Where Have You Been?" (Oates, 1966) versus several other interpretations of the same work. It takes a lot to get to me, but this story was the most upsetting piece of literature I have ever read in my entire life. In my opinion, the ending of the story was just horrific. I searched on the Internet, trying to find others' analysis of WAYGWHYB ["Where Are You Going, Where Have You Been"], and found a number of sites that "obviously had it all wrong" [in my opinion]. I had to face the reality that I was the one who interpreted the piece in a way that was inconsistent with all the other readers, and therefore, I was the one off base, perhaps misinterpreting the text. Why? As with any life experience, we all bring our own circumstances, history and thoughts with us when we read a piece of literature; we mix it all together, and out comes our personal interpretation. I had a particularly upsetting set of circumstances when I was in college some 20 years ago. I am a fighter, strong, independent, etc., but when I was put into one, specific bad spot, I actually froze—could not move nor speak; I just stood there. When I read the portion of the story where Connie finds herself out of her own control and in Arnold's control, because of my personal history (and the thoughts and fears that stemmed from that history), I was almost transported back in time to my situation, therefore severely influencing my interpretation of the piece.
>
> After reading "A Psychological Analysis of Connie" (Kurkowski, n.d.), I began to understand Oates' intentions a bit better and could look at WAYGWHYB through different eyes. Of course, I did not really consider Kurkowski's interpretation closer to the intent of the writer until I had read a number of analyses that all concurred, such as "The Influence of Heritage and Social Milieu," by Kerstin Heist (n.d.). Therefore, if Oates was going for an "ambiguous conclusion, which allows for several interpretations of the story's meaning," she definitely wrote an effective piece of literature (http://www.enotes.com, para 2). I would be interested in knowing who else out there in e–mail land read this story, and what do you think happened when Connie went with Arnold? The story ending that seemed very clear to me was that she was going to be raped and murdered. I am glad that others did not see it ending that way!

References

Heist, K. (n.d.). The influence of heritage and social milieu. Retrieved from http://www.enotes.com/where–are/

Kurkowski, C. J. (n.d.). Psychological analysis of Connie: A feminist viewpoint of "Where are you going, where have you been?" Retrieved from http://home.mind-spring.com/~blkgrnt/footlights/foot66.html

Oates, J. C. (1966). Where are you going, where have you been? As published in Oates, J. C. (1970). *The wheel of love and other stories*. New York, NY: Fawcett Crest Books.

Notice that this discussion post is very engaged with the material, offers personal insights, and takes a critical approach to the texts. A thoughtful discussion post may involve showing a change in one's interpretation, as the one above does. Discussion posts are typically evaluated according to a rubric (see Table 2.3 for a sample). The grade that you receive on your discussion post will likely be based on these sorts of criteria. However, if the post uses correct grammar but does not in any way reply to the instructor's question, it will not be considered an adequate response.

Table 2.3: Sample discussion-post rubric

Critical Thinking Skills/ Original Thoughts	Student applies relevant, professional, personal, or other real-world experiences in a manner that is rich in thought and provides valuable insight into the topic.
Content/Subject Knowledge	Student thoroughly addresses all elements of the discussion prompt, and demonstrates an advanced knowledge of the topic. Student makes strong and precise connections to previous and/or current course content, or to real-life situations, in initial post.
Participation	Student responds with thorough and constructive analysis to the required number of peers, relating the response to relevant course concepts. Student may pose pertinent follow-up thoughts or questions about the topic, and demonstrates respect for the diverse opinions of fellow learners.
Coherence and Organization	Student effectively communicates a central idea or point that is weaved throughout the entirety of the post, in a coherent and logical manner. Post is easy to understand.
Mechanics	Initial post contains very few, if any, minor errors related to grammar, spelling, and sentence structure. Post is easy to read and understand. Student properly cites resources (if applicable), per instructor expectations.

The previous discussion post example was given an exemplary grade by the instructor because it excelled in fulfilling each of the requirements outlined in Table 2.3. Understanding what the post is asking of you is the most important thing. Make sure that the assignment is clear to you before you begin and ask for clarification if you need it. Note that if your instructor does not ask you to directly reply to other postings, this will likely not be a part of the grading rubric for that assignment.

Reading and Understanding Assignments

Remember that to earn the highest possible grade on a discussion assignment, you must cover all of the key areas. The feature *Writing Samples: Examples of a Discussion-Post Assignment* shows an example of a discussion-post assignment, with the key words and phrases and action verbs underlined and listed.

Writing Samples: Examples of a Discussion-Post Assignment

Example: Select a philosophy of education that is most like your own from Chapter 3 (Idealism, Realism, Neo-Thomism, Pragmatism, or Existentialism) and describe it using one other source in addition to the text. Explain how the chosen philosophy is most like your own.

List of Key Words and Phrases
- select
- philosophy of education
- most like your own
- from Chapter 3
- describe it
- using one other source in addition to the text
- Explain how the chosen philosophy is most like your own.

List of Action Verbs
- select
- describe
- explain

Then, before you submit your written assignment, go back and check your list to make sure you have addressed each one.

The example in *Writing in Action: Example of a Discussion-Post Assignment* asks you to find the action verbs and the corresponding objectives and requirements for those verbs in Table 2.2 and determine the assignment requirements.

Writing in Action: Example of a Discussion-Post Assignment

Example: Write a two- to three-page narrative essay that describes a special event or occasion in your life. Make sure you state the purpose and location of the event or occasion, identify the people who attended, and explain why this event or occasion was important to you. Your paper must have a title page, formatted in proper APA style, as shown in your style guide.

List of Key Words and Phrases

-
-
-
-
-
-

List of Action Verbs

-
-
-
-
-
-

Note especially that the assignment asks the student to write about a special occasion or event. This may seem minor, but it is not. If a well-intentioned student writes a summary of several special events that occurred while he or she was growing up, that would not be an adequate response to the assignment. The assignment wants the writer to focus on one specific event, in part because doing so teaches writers how to focus on one moment and how to amplify the scene with details. If the student writes about two or three events instead of just one, he or she will likely end up summarizing these events, and there will be far fewer details in the writing. Also make sure that you always answer each part of the assignment. Reread the assignment several times, marking it carefully, to make sure you understand all of the tasks the assignment is requiring you to complete.

Assignment Grading

Your college assignments will likely be graded on (1) what you wrote and how well you wrote it, (2) to what degree you responded to all key words and phrases and performed the requirements of the action verbs in the assignment, and (3) to what extent your paper is grammatically correct and to what degree your paper adheres to the required documentation guidelines or other formatting instructions given by your teacher. Please note that your instructors will weigh these various elements differently. While some instructors may specifically ask students to focus more on Step 1 for a particular assignment, others may focus more on Step 2. Students should ask instructors about these guidelines and which the instructor will weigh more heavily.

2.4 Critical Reading: Putting It Into Practice

In order to become a critical reader, practice is absolutely essential. Students should consciously practice critical reading skills with each reading and writing assignment. In this section, you will find several critical reading exercises to get you started on practicing these essential skills.

Critical Reading Exercise: Ralph Waldo Emerson

Below is an excerpt from Ralph Waldo Emerson's *Nature*. As you read, try to use the active reading strategies discussed earlier in this chapter. Do not forget to use the electronic notation and highlight tools. From the title of the text, you can approach it by asking yourself: "What is Emerson's definition of nature? Why and how is it important for him?" Emerson writes:

> In inquiries respecting the laws of the world and the frame of things, the highest reason is always the truest. That which seems faintly possible—it is so refined, is often faint and dim because it is deepest seated in the mind among the eternal verities. Empirical science is apt to cloud the sight, and, by the very knowledge of functions and processes, to bereave the student of the manly contemplation of the whole. (1849/1996, p. 43)

mimagephotography/Shutterstock.com

What are Emerson's views on nature? How would you define it, and why do you think nature is so important to humans?

Exercise #1: After reading the excerpt from Emerson, write an essay in which you discuss what Emerson says about nature, and how he defines it. After giving a definition for nature, describe what Emerson says hinders our understanding of nature. Then relate this to how nature seems to be important to the human. Write an essay of approximately two to three pages in answer to this question.

Although reading more from Emerson would add to your understanding of this excerpt, you could still answer the assignment questions above based on the lines you have been given. Begin by looking up unfamiliar words, such as "inquiries," "verities," and "empirical." Then proceed toward working through an understanding of the paragraph. The more you practice active reading strategies, the more your reading abilities will be strengthened.

Critical Reading Exercise: Sophocles

This chapter included an excerpt from Sophocles's *Antigone*, an example that offered some insight into what fathers—particularly kings—think about the significance of sons. By contrast, there are also several moments of the play in which female characters make statements about their role as women in Greek society. With the previous example in mind (in which King Creon emphasizes the significance of sons for war) think about another excerpt from the play, as stated by the female protagonist Antigone. She explains why she is utterly devoted to the idea of giving her dead brother a proper burial:

> [I]f I had been the mother of children/or if my husband died, exposed and rotting—/I'd never have taken this ordeal upon myself,/never defied our people's will. . . . A husband dead, there might have been another./A child by another too, if I had lost the first./But mother and father both lost in the halls of Death,/no brother could ever spring to light again. (1984, pp. 996–1004)

Exercise #2: Antigone explains that the death of her brother, Polyneices, makes her feel obligated to give him a proper burial. King Creon, who views Polyneices as a traitor, has ordered that he should not be buried. Antigone, however, suggests that giving her brother Polyneices a proper burial is an extremely personally significant act to her. Write an essay of two full pages in length in which you discuss why, if her brother is so important to her, in this passage she says she would not bury a dead husband or child? Why would this character place her brother as the most significant family relationship?

Begin by pulling out the key words and phrases that seem most striking to you. Why would Antigone have this strong devotion to her brother? Is it possibly related to the fact that her parents are dead, so "no brother could ever spring to light again?" Analyze the language Antigone uses and develop a well-supported response to the question.

Chapter Summary

Reading carefully is crucial for both the writing and the learning process as a student. Reading a text very carefully the first time through will put you in a good position to write an effective response or essay about that text. Conversely, skimming a text leads to vague summaries and a lack of analysis. Practice each of the strategies for active reading whenever you read a text, essay prompt, or discussion-post assignment—and even, of course, while you are reading this text. Noting key words, phrases, and verbs that seem particularly important is an essential step in the critical reading process and will help you with anything you read. Use the practice exercises in the previous section to begin working on directly applying reading skills and methods to your writing.

Key Terms

active reading A series of strategies that help you engage with a text, including highlighting and circling key terms, writing question marks and exclamation points, and writing notes in the margins of the text.

annotating Writing a note—in the margin of the document you are reading or on a separate piece of paper—that explains or comments on what you have read.

bibliography A list of books referenced in a text that appears toward the end of the material.

brainstorming Summarizing your main ideas, questions, and responses to a text you are reading in order to try to find main points. This process can help you organize your thoughts before writing a first draft of a paper.

index A list, usually toward the end of a text, that includes the names of authors, themes, and concepts covered in the text. It is a guide that tells you what the text covers and gives page numbers that correspond to that entry.

reading journal A space where readers organize thoughts and questions about a text. It may include definitions of words that needed to be looked up, reflections on the text, or questions about moments in the text that are not clearly resolved or that seem perplexing.

SQ3R method A useful strategy for reading books and other lengthy reading materials. SQ3R is an abbreviation for Survey, Question, Read, Recite, and Review.

College Writing

3

michaeljung/Shutterstock.com

Learning Objectives

After reading this chapter, you should be able to do the following:

1. Recognize the common purposes and types of college writing.

2. Explain the elements of the personal college essay, including its purpose, supporting evidence types, and subjective writing style.

3. Summarize the elements of the expository essay, including its purpose, style, and objective nature.

4. Compare the elements of persuasive, argumentative, research, and combination college essays.

5. Identify the elements of research writing.

6. Identify the elements of combination papers.

7. Define the meaning of the writer's voice, including the difference between formal and informal language, plagiarism, and self-revision.

Never give up. And most importantly, be true to yourself. Write from your heart, in your own voice, and about what you believe in.

—Louise Brown

From *Essentials of College Writing: Contemporary Applications, 2/E* by Christine M. Connell and Kathy Sole. © 2013 Bridgepoint Education.

Different types of writing assignments will have a different purpose, audience, and focus, and this chapter offers a discussion of the different types of writing you will likely be asked to do in your college courses. Each of the main genres of writing this chapter discusses—personal writing, expository writing, persuasive and argumentative writing, and research papers—is essential for your college courses, but each also translates beyond the classroom. The chances are great that you will use elements of these different types of writing in any profession or in your personal life, from writing a proposal for a project to emailing a friend. Writing is a direct expression of thinking and is therefore a powerful tool for helping you communicate. Fully understanding your writing assignments is the first step toward writing a strong essay, avoiding common pitfalls, and learning how to use this powerful tool.

3.1 The Purpose and Types of College Writing

College writing is generally not meant to commemorate or to entertain. You may be required in your college courses to write academic papers for any of these four purposes:

- To tell a story or to share personal opinions or experiences
- To inform, explain, explore, analyze, or interpret ideas
- To convince readers to share your point of view about a subject or to take some action you recommend
- To acquire knowledge and/or to organize, analyze, and synthesize information.

Sometimes an assignment will have more than one purpose and require a paper that combines two or more of these purposes, such as sharing information and persuading the reader.

The Purpose of College Writing

Learning some of the fundamentals of college writing will not simply help you in this course—it will also help give you the skills you will need to write in other types of college courses. Most college courses—from English composition to chemistry—require some writing and the ability to read and correctly interpret assignments. Even if you do not want a career in a humanities-related field, improving your writing skills will help you become a more effective communicator and thinker.

Types of College Writing

Your college papers can be classified into four different types: (1) personal writing, (2) exposition, (3) persuasion and argument, and (4) research papers. As we discussed, some of your college assignments will require one specific type of writing or another, and some may be a combination of two or more of these four types. An important aspect of developing your college writing skills is to understand when to use which type of academic writing. If you clearly understand each of the four types of college writing, you will be able to "switch gears" when necessary to complete your assignments correctly. If you are uncertain about the type of writing an assignment requires, make sure you ask your instructor or teaching assistant to clarify it for you.

Regardless of which type of paper you are preparing, remember that college writing tends to use formal language and generally avoids slang, jargon, and contractions. You must also write your papers in complete sentences; organize your writing into logical paragraphs; use proper capitalization, grammar, and punctuation; and use language that is clear and not overly emotional. We will examine all four types of college writing in detail in later chapters. However, a brief overview of each type is provided in the following sections, and the chart in Figure 3.1 summarizes each type of college writing. You might want to print this chart to keep for reference in your future college courses.

Figure 3.1: Types of college papers

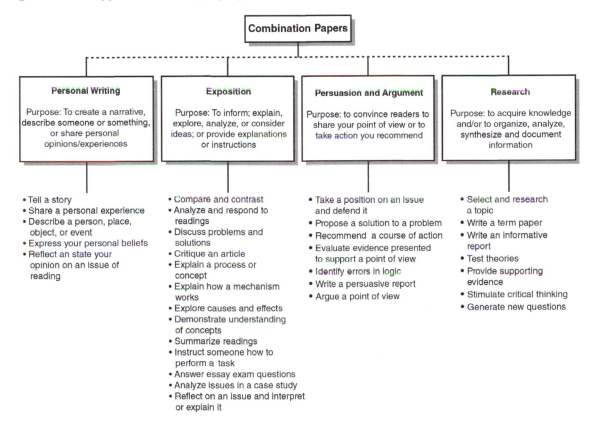

Combination Papers

Personal Writing

Purpose: To create a narrative, describe someone or something, or share personal opinions/experiences

- Tell a story
- Share a personal experience
- Describe a person, place, object, or event
- Express your personal beliefs
- Reflect an state your opinion on an issue of reading

Exposition

Purpose: To inform; explain, explore, analyze, or consider ideas; or provide explanations or instructions

- Compare and contrast
- Analyze and respond to readings
- Discuss problems and solutions
- Critique an article
- Explain a process or concept
- Explain how a mechanism works
- Explore causes and effects
- Demonstrate understanding of concepts
- Summarize readings
- Instruct someone how to perform a task
- Answer essay exam questions
- Analyze issues in a case study
- Reflect on an issue and interpret or explain it

Persuasion and Argument

Purpose: to convince readers to share your point of view or to take action you recommend

- Take a position on an issue and defend it
- Propose a solution to a problem
- Recommend a course of action
- Evaluate evidence presented to support a point of view
- Identify errors in logic
- Write a persuasive report
- Argue a point of view

Research

Purpose: to acquire knowledge and/or to organize, analyze, synthesize and document information

- Select and research a topic
- Write a term paper
- Write an informative report
- Test theories
- Provide supporting evidence
- Stimulate critical thinking
- Generate new questions

3.2 Personal Writing

Writing assignments that ask you to state your opinion about an issue; to document your observations; to relate a subject to your own life; to share a story; or to provide a description of a person, place, object, or event call for **personal writing**. Personal opinion and narrative essays fall into this category, as do some reflective papers, which ask students to reflect on a subject's meaning to them or to relate it to a personal experience. Personal writing is **subjective**, or based on your own observation, experience, or opinion. If you have ever written a paper about what you did on your summer vacation or given your opinion about an issue, you have written a personal paper. Personal writing asks *what you think* about a subject or *what you observed or experienced.*

Recognizing a Personal Writing Assignment

Remember to make sure that you read your assignments carefully and review key words and action verbs to determine whether you are being asked to write a personal paper, an expository paper, a persuasive paper, a research paper, or some combination of these types of college writing. You can often recognize a persuasive writing assignment by key words or phrases in the assignment that ask you for your opinion or views on a subject.

mimagephotography/Shutterstock.com

Writing about a recent vacation is a common subject for personal writing.

Table 3.1 shows some examples of key words and phrases that usually signal a personal paper.

Table 3.1: Examples of personal paper key words and phrases

Relate an experience you have had . . .	Describe an event in which you . . .
Recall a situation . . .	Identify a time when . . .
How do you believe we can we solve . . .	Why do you think . . .
What is your opinion about . . .	How would you have handled . . .

Writing in Action: Examples of Personal Paper Assignments provides some examples of assignments from actual college courses that would require a personal paper. Notice that each assignment asks you to give your opinion about a subject, to share incidents from your life, or to relate an issue to your own experiences. You can recognize a personal paper assignment by these characteristics. See *Writing in Action: Examining a Personal Writing Prompt* at the end of this section for further explanation of how to recognize and interpret these characteristics in a personal writing prompt.

Writing in Action: Examples of Personal Paper Assignments

Key words and action verbs are underlined in the following examples:

- Write about an <u>experience</u> in which <u>you struggled with something</u> and <u>were unsuccessful</u> and <u>discuss what you learned</u> from the experience.
- <u>Explain what you think</u> about a <u>current scientific</u> or <u>social controversy.</u>
- <u>Reflect</u> on a <u>person</u> who <u>had a strong impact on your life</u> and the <u>ways</u> in which <u>he or she influenced you.</u>
- <u>Imagine</u> that <u>you have unlimited wealth</u> and write about <u>what you would do</u> with <u>your money</u> and <u>why.</u>
- <u>What</u> do <u>you think</u> has been the <u>most important social or political movement</u> of the <u>20th century</u>?

Writing in Action: Examining a Personal Writing Prompt

Write a <u>two- to three-page paper</u> in which you <u>relate an experience</u> you have had <u>communicating</u> with someone from a different culture.

The key phrase "relate an experience you have had" should alert you to the fact that this assignment is to tell a personal story. Since the verb "communicating" seems to be the main action verb, this should draw your attention toward thinking about a significant communication experience or interaction you had with someone from another culture. It would be useful to select a communication experience that was about an interesting subject of some depth. Since changes in story lines or turning points are always helpful with a personal narrative essay, selecting an experience in which initial communication trouble was somehow overcome could be a very interesting approach to the assignment.

Characteristics of Personal Writing

What distinguishes personal writing from other types of college writing is that your goal is not to present information you learned from the course text or from other outside sources; instead, it is to present your own thoughts, perspectives, beliefs, opinions, views, emotions, or experiences. In a personal paper, you may include facts you obtained through research to support your statements; however, you are not usually required to do so. You are, however, required to clearly explain and support your personal views.

In personal papers, you are the speaker, so the use of the pronouns *I, me, my, mine, we,* or *our* is expected. These pronouns are known as first-person pronouns, so this type of writing is said to be from a first-person point of view. In personal papers, you are also speaking directly to your readers, so the use of the pronouns *you* or *your*, which are called second-person pronouns, is also permitted. In personal writing, you must state your position or opinion on an issue and support your point of view with reasons, examples, personal anecdotes, illustrations, or stories. Below is an example of a paragraph from a personal paper about growing vegetables.

> I learned to grow a vegetable garden when I was a young child. Every spring, my mother and I would work together to prepare the vegetable beds. Then, I would plant the seeds according to the directions on the back of each vegetable seed package. I would look forward to checking the garden each day. When the seeds began to sprout, I always thought it was magical.

This paragraph conveys the inner experiences of the writer, and that is usually desired in personal essays. It discusses a personal experience but also gives the reader a sense about the narrator as a young person who was delighted by the seemingly "magical" nature of seedlings beginning to sprout.

3.3 Expository Writing

xposition, or **expository writing**, shares information or explains a subject to readers. You may have prior knowledge of a subject that you communicate to readers, or you may be required to write a combination paper in which you share your own ideas along with information you found by conducting research on the topic. Writing assignments that ask you to compare and contrast two ideas, discuss problems and solutions, critique an article you have read, explain a concept or a process, write a report, summarize what you have learned, or analyze issues all require an expository paper.

Rawpixel.com/Shutterstock.com

Expository writing is often essential in the workplace to convey ideas and concepts to your coworkers.

Recognizing an Expository Writing Assignment

Exposition is involved in a wide range of different kinds of papers that are written for a variety of different reasons. However, you can recognize expository writing because its primary purpose is always to inform readers about a subject. You can often identify an expository writing prompt from the key words shown in Table 3.2.

Table 3.2: Examples of key words and phrases for expository papers

Discuss the theory of . . .	Summarize the key concepts . . .
Reflect on how this concept could be applied . . .	Explain the cause of . . .
Demonstrate your understanding of . . .	Describe the advantages and disadvantages of . . .
Compare and contrast different views of . . .	Analyze the effects of . . .
Interpret the passage shown below and support your conclusions . . .	Define . . .
Evaluate the possible effects of . . .	Summarize the key concepts in the chapter and discuss their importance . . .

The following features give an example of an expository writing assignment (*Writing in Action: Expository Writing*) and a breakdown of an expository writing prompt (*Writing in Action: Examining an Expository Writing Prompt*).

Writing in Action: Expository Writing

Write a rough draft for your final paper in which you compare and contrast two literary works from this course that share the same theme (using the "Themes & Corresponding Works" list in the Week Five Final Paper instructions as a guide).

Assignment Requirements
    a. **Theme**: Your paper must address one of the themes listed.
    b. **Length**: Your draft should be six to ten double-spaced pages in length (excluding title and reference page)
    c. **Sources**: Utilize at least six scholarly sources to support your thesis (including the course text and at least two sources from your college library).
    d. **Formatting**: Your draft must be formatted to your course's specified documentation style.

The paper must be six to ten pages in length (excluding the title and reference page), and formatted according to your course's specified documentation style. You must use at least six scholarly resources (at least two of which can be found in your college library) other than the textbook to support your claims and subclaims. Cite your resources in text and on the reference page.

The paper should be organized around your thesis. When developing a thesis for a comparative paper, consider how a comparison of the works provides deeper insight into the topic of your paper (i.e., think about why you have chosen to look at these particular works in relation to one another). In your analysis, consider the relationships among the following elements:

    a. Content
    b. Form (e.g., short story vs. poem)
    c. Style

Writing in Action: Examining an Expository Essay Prompt

Write a two-to-three-page paper in which you discuss the communication issues that can arise in a conversation with someone from another culture.

This more formal writing assignment does not ask you to share a personal story or experience. The key phrase "discuss the communication issues that can arise" reveals that the assignment requires sharing information with readers about these issues. This is an expository essay assignment, asking you to discuss a potential communication issue, likely written in the third person. In this assignment, the communication issue can be an imagined, theoretical conversation. It would likely include a thesis statement that indicates the significance of the communication issues you discuss.

Types and Characteristics of Expository Writing

You have a great responsibility when you write expository papers. Remember that expository writing often explains or clarifies information and, in the workplace, information in expository papers may be used for decision making. Readers are depending on you to give them information that is accurate, complete, clear, and focused. One of the most important characteristics of effective exposition is that it must tell readers what they need to know. To accomplish this goal, you must adequately plan what you intend to cover, analyze the needs of your audience, and ensure that you have covered all requirements of the assignment.

Discussion Questions and Posts

As we discussed in Chapter 2, if your course requires discussion posts, they should be considered formal college writing assignments. If a discussion assignment calls for you to provide your personal views on a subject in addition to analyzing a subject, treat the assignment as you would a "mini" expository paper. Structure your response to the discussion assignment with a short introduction, body, and conclusion, and incorporate the characteristics of a personal paper discussed in this chapter.

Discussion posts simulate class discussions, so your language and writing style do not have to be as formal as in your written papers. However, you must write your discussion posts in complete sentences and in paragraph form. Your posts should also be grammatically correct, punctuated and capitalized properly, and proofread. For lengthy posts, create your post first in a word processing program, such as Microsoft Word®. Then you can revise, edit, proofread, and save it until you are satisfied with the final version. At that point, you can copy and paste it into the course discussion area.

When you are responding to a discussion post that calls for personal writing, always respond to others' posts with a respectful tone even if you strongly disagree. State whether you agree or disagree with the point of view expressed and explain why you agree or disagree. You may also respond to the posts of other students by sharing a personal insight you gained or a fact you learned from reading your peer's post. Explain how that information helped you understand the issue or made you rethink your own views.

Written Assignments

When you write expository papers, do not assume that the reader has prior knowledge or understanding of the topic; always provide some brief background information to introduce your subject. Then, determine the main points you must include in your paper and proceed to cover them in a logical and organized manner. Expository writing should be **objective**, or based on facts. Unlike personal or persuasive writing, you should not share your personal opinion about the topic or judge the information you present. Your task is simply to present it as fairly and accurately as you can. Because expository writing focuses on the subject matter, it generally uses a third-person point of view (*he, she, they, the subject, the author*). The example below illustrates an expository paragraph about growing vegetables.

> Growing vegetables requires planting seeds or seedlings (which are small plants) in the garden, when no threat of frost exists. Small seedlings are tender and can be easily damaged when their fine roots are exposed to air or disturbed during the transplanting process. This condition, known as "transplant shock," can prevent the plants from thriving in their new environment or may even kill them. To prevent transplant shock, seedlings should be watered with a solution of vitamin B-1 immediately after they are planted.

This paragraph is an objective account of how to maximize the growth potential of seedlings. It does not express the writer's emotions about plants growing; it seeks to give the reader concrete information.

To understand exposition more thoroughly, go to http://www.newyorker.com/archive/2005/12/19/051219fa_fact1 and read *Becoming Mary Poppins* by Caitlin Flanagan (2005) that illustrates this type of writing.

Notice that although Flanagan is writing from her own viewpoint, this is not a personal essay. The focus of the essay is not on the author's experiences, opinions, or emotional reactions; it is on the subjects of the paper—the Mary Poppins movie, P. L. Travers, and Walt Disney. The primary purpose of the writing is to provide readers with information and commentary about the movie and about these individuals.

3.4 Persuasive and Argumentative Writing

Persuasion is an attempt to influence others to adopt a certain belief or point of view or to convince them to take some action. As you will recall from Chapter 1, persuasion may take the form of one of three different appeals to the reader—pathos, ethos, and logos. Persuasion broadly encompasses using any rhetorical strategies to sway an audience. Whenever we attempt to get others to accept our opinion on a subject, to agree with our point of view on an issue, or to take some action we recommend, we are engaged in persuasion. Argument is a specific type of persuasive writing in which you follow a structured process for persuading others, primarily through logical reasoning (logos). Argument is one method of persuasion that intends to convey a developed reason to support what it is trying to persuade an audience to do or think. Persuasion, on the other hand, may rely more on an audience's emotions (pathos), rather than on reasoning, and persuasion

Everett Collection/Shutterstock.com

Politicians use persuasive and argumentative writing in their campaign speeches and debates in order to sway undecided voters to their side of the issues.

may not have a well-developed set of reasons. For instance, a TV commercial may suggest that you should buy a particular car because it is attractive to members of the opposite sex. The commercial would be an example of persuasion because it uses emotion rather than logic as its primary strategy.

Recognizing Persuasive and Argumentative Writing Assignments

Persuasive and argumentative papers frequently deal with controversial subjects, issues that are in dispute, or topics on which two or more positions exist. When you are asked to take a stand or a position on an issue, to defend your opinion on a subject, to evaluate a position other people have advocated to determine whether it is logical or desirable, to study a problem and propose a solution to it, or to construct an argument, a persuasive or argument paper is required.

You can often recognize a persuasive writing assignment by the key words shown in Table 3.3 and an argument paper by the key words shown in Table 3.4.

Table 3.3: Key words and phrases for a persuasive paper

Do you agree with the statement that . . .	Consider whether . . .
What is your opinion about . . .	Provide your views on . . .

Table 3.4: Key words and phrases for an argument paper

Give arguments for and against . . .	Evaluate the options/alternative . . .
What are the advantages and disadvantages of . . .	Discuss . . . and present evidence to support your argument.

Notice that the prompt in *Writing in Action: Examining a Persuasive Essay Prompt* asks you to take a position and convince your audience to accept *your* point of view. This type of wording should alert you to the type of essay the prompt is asking you to write.

Writing in Action: Examining a Persuasive Essay Prompt

Write a two- to three-page paper in which you take a position on a *controversial* issue and attempt to convince the audience to accept your point of view.

In this instance, the primary purpose of the assignment is to persuade the audience to accept your point of view about a controversial issue, so it is calling for a persuasive essay. This essay should be written in the third person and use a formal tone throughout. It requires an extensive thesis and detailed main points with evidence to support each of these points.

Characteristics of Persuasive Writing

Persuasive papers and argument papers are two types of persuasive writing. They are similar in that their purpose is to influence others; however, they are different in the way they endeavor to do this. When you attempt to persuade someone, you try to change that person's mind by convincing him or her that your point of view is correct. Thus, you provide a one-sided discussion of the issue in which your point of view is the primary point you want to make. Persuasion is based on your personal conviction that your way of thinking is the right way. Sometimes this is accomplished through **appeals to emotion**, or attempts to create an emotional response in the audience in order to persuade that audience to do or believe something. Although persuasive papers can include appeals to emotion, you should always consider what effect this might have on your audience.

Persuasive and argument writing may use a variety of approaches to achieve their purposes. These papers are often written using a third-person point of view to keep the writing focused on the issue, and they use logic to appeal to readers. However, in some papers, you may want to engage readers in the discussion, so you may talk to them directly using a second-person point of view (*you, your*) or create a bond with them by using a first-person plural point of view (*we, our*). The following paragraph from a persuasive paper shows how these different approaches can be combined:

> Planting vegetables in a home garden can be an exciting and satisfying hobby. It can be gratifying to serve your homegrown vegetables at family meals or to share your harvest with neighbors. Not only is it fun to watch the plants mature and to inspect the progress of the vegetables as they grow, but the taste of homegrown vegetables cannot be beat. While others are buying tasteless hothouse tomatoes at the grocery store this summer, you could be harvesting vine-ripened tomatoes from your own backyard.

This paragraph attempts to persuade the reader that planting vegetables is a worthwhile hobby. It gives reasons why one should plant vegetables and is trying to encourage the reader to plant a vegetable garden. Note that this persuasive example is not about a controversial issue, but persuasive essays frequently are about controversial topics.

Characteristics of Argumentative Writing

Argument is concerned with proving a point, and argument papers usually require research to gather evidence in order to do so. Argument papers require that you carefully consider the information you will use from your research. You must make sure to address all sides of the issue and present it in an organized way that is easy for your readers to follow. Your job is to show your readers that you are well informed, that you have a good understanding of the issue, that you have considered different points of view, and that, after careful consideration, you have decided that the point of view you advocate is the correct one.

While you are working on your argument paper, keep in mind that conducting research, thinking, and writing happen simultaneously. As you gather information, take notes, and think about what you are learning, you begin to get a clearer picture of the issue. You must usually consider points of view other than your own and gather evidence to refute these points. In conducting this research, you may even find that you change your position on the issue, based on the evidence you found. In an argument, in addition to outlining your viewpoint on an issue, you must establish your credibility, usually through your research. You convince readers to accept your point of view by the force of your evidence.

3.5 Writing Research Papers

Research writing requires you to write about a subject using information you gather from outside sources. These types of assignments may also be called *term papers*, *informative* or *analytical reports*, or *case studies*. When you write a research paper, imagine yourself as a scientist or an investigative reporter trying to uncover the facts. You must remain objective and not form an opinion or force the information to fit your preconceived ideas. Remember that you are engaged in a search to find the answer to the question, "What is the truth about this subject?"

Writing a research paper requires that you gather information and organize that information until a picture begins to emerge. You might think of research

Gorodenkoff/Shutterstock.com

Much in the same way scientists perform research in order to support their hypotheses, when writing a research paper, you must gather enough evidence to support the assertion you are trying to make.

or analytical writing as a jigsaw puzzle in which you search for pieces of a puzzle and put them together in a logical way to form a conclusion. Research papers also require you to critically evaluate an issue or to compare two or more theories or systems. You may start out with an idea of what you think you might find (called a hypothesis), but you must keep an open mind, suspend judgment, follow the evidence, and see where it leads you.

Recognizing Research Paper Assignments

Research papers are used throughout a variety of disciplines, so it is important to be able to recognize when an assignment requires you to conduct research writing. Whenever a prompt asks you to substantiate a claim using outside resources, and not personal opinion, you should recognize this as a direction to write a research paper. *Writing in Action: Research Writing* provides an example of a research writing assignment.

Writing in Action: Research Writing

Capstone Research Paper for Social and Criminal Justice

You will submit an appropriate project focused upon a contemporary criminal justice issue. Students are encouraged to use multimedia, scholarly sources, interviews with professionals in the field, and primary sources to identify and devise a workable plan to solve a modern criminal justice issue. At a minimum, a successful project will devise strategies focused upon all of the learning objectives for the criminal justice program.

The student will:

1. Examine law-enforcement issues.
2. Apply knowledge of socio-economic (cultural) diversity to criminal justice.
3. Understand the U.S. Constitution and the application of criminal and social justice theories through the Constitution.
4. Investigate the operation of the criminal justice system.
5. Explore crime scene investigation techniques: crime scene security and the collection, preservation, and presentation of evidence.
6. Study correctional institutions and the criminal and social justice aspects of incarceration and release issues.
7. Understand the centralization of criminal justice agencies domestically, the U.S. Homeland Security Act, and the international aspects of criminal and social justice.
8. Examine the relationship of social justice to the criminal justice system.
9. Apply information from sociology, law, psychology, ethics, and related fields to the study of criminal justice.
10. Solve a modern criminal and social justice issue through a comprehensive capstone course.

Students can supplement their projects with any of the following: all scholarly sources, including documentaries and contemporary news-reporting; comparisons of similar tactics/agencies in varying situations and their effects; political and military trends and technology that directly impact the tactics/organizations being influenced. The finished paper must be at least 20 pages in length and include no fewer than five scholarly resources.

Characteristics of Research Papers

When you write a research paper, your purpose is to share with readers the information you found in outside sources about your topic. As a scientist or an investigator, you simply report the facts; you do not add your personal opinion. In this type of writing, the conclusion you reach is the one supported by the facts you found in your research. The following is an example of a paragraph from this type of paper:

> Growing summer vegetables in the Pacific Northwest is challenging. Tomatoes, for example, thrive in warm weather, and most do not fare well when nighttime temperatures fall below 55 degrees Fahrenheit (Wilson, 2012). Pacific Northwest summer evening temperatures are often below this threshold. Gardeners can count on nighttime temperatures consistently above 55 degrees only about 2 weeks of the year (Yardley, 2013). However, gardeners can have success if they choose the right tomato varieties for this climate and correctly time the planting of their tomato seedlings.

This excerpt from a research essay is using sources to support its claim. There is research that was found in outside sources that helps substantiate the claims the writer makes.

3.6 Writing Combination Papers

So far in this chapter, we have outlined the individual types of writing you will encounter in this and other college courses. However, some assignments may ask you to write a paper using a combination of these types. For example, an assignment asking you to write on genetically modified foods may require you to discuss an issue (expository), take a position on that issue, and convince the reader to accept your viewpoint (persuasive) by providing evidence from research to support your position (research). Always read assignments carefully and list key words and phrases to ensure that you thoroughly understand the assignment requirements.

Recognizing Combination Paper Assignments

You may find that some of your college assignments require you to gather information on a controversial issue, present this information in a fair and balanced manner, make a decision to choose one side or another, and defend your choice. These assignments require a paper that is a combination of expository writing and research; they include papers such as proposals, position papers, and some case studies. In these assignments, you must objectively search for and present information, and then take a personal stand on one side of the issue and defend your choice. *Writing in Action: Examining a Combination Writing Prompt* illustrates the type of prompt you may see when writing a combination paper.

Writing in Action: Examining a Combination Writing Prompt

Write a two- to three-page paper in which you present a problem and recommend a solution to this problem.

This assignment is asking you to fulfill two different purposes. First, you must share information by presenting a problem, as you would in an expository essay. Then you must "recommend a solution to this problem," which means attempting to convince or persuade your reader to accept your proposed solution. This part of the prompt calls for an argument essay because it requires formulating an interpretation and concrete argument that is a solution to the problem you discuss.

Characteristics of Combination Papers

The introduction of this type of paper (in which you discuss the subject you have chosen and why you have selected it) and the conclusion (in which you make the recommendation and defend it) may be written in either first person or third person. Make certain you understand which your instructor requires. In the body of the paper, objectively report the information you have gleaned from your research. An example of this type of combination paper would be if you were asked to conduct research on types of tomatoes and to recommend the type readers should plant. The following is an example of such a paper that combines some of the information in the preceding research example with a specific recommendation:

> Growing summer vegetables in the Pacific Northwest is challenging. Tomatoes, for example, thrive in warm weather, and most do not fare well when nighttime temperatures fall below 55 degrees Fahrenheit (Wilson, 2012), as is often the case during summer in this region. However, gardeners can have success if they choose the right tomato varieties for this climate. One type of tomato grows particularly well in the Pacific Northwest: Sungold. The Sungold tomato is a large, golden, cherry-type tomato that thrives in cooler climates (Yardley, 2013). A local horticulturist, who has grown tomatoes in the region for 15 years, recommends this variety on his website http://www.localhorticulture.com, and I can personally recommend this tomato as well. I have grown Sungold for the past 2 years with great success. The plants have no problem with the cool nighttime summers here, and Sungold has a shorter growing season than most other tomato varieties (Wilson, 2012). An added bonus is that the plants continue to produce well into the fall when other varieties have gone to seed. I have found this variety to be the best choice for consistent growth and great taste in my Pacific Northwest garden.

This paper is simultaneously relying on research and persuasion to convey a purpose. The paragraph is relying on information from an outside source and is also using that information to persuade the reader to plant Sungold tomatoes if you live in the Pacific Northwest.

3.7 The Writer's Voice

Another important element in effective college writing is the paper's writing style and what it conveys about the writer. Writing is not just a mechanical process; it is also an art. Every piece of writing is a personal undertaking, and every piece of writing is unique. When we write, we interact with the audience in our own way, and this interaction helps create and shape the content, style, mood, and tone of our writing. This unique manner of writing creates what is known as the writer's style, including both the writer's tone and writer's voice (Ruddell, 1997).

Understanding Tone and Voice

Our language choices, including decisions about tone and voice, give our written work a unique character. Although tone and voice are interrelated, they are two distinct terms. **Tone** refers to the mood or attitude the writer conveys toward the subject matter. Some examples of tone include critical, humorous, ironic, serious, formal, informal, and many other attitudes represented in the writing. For instance, the overall tone of this book is formal, but if the entire book were completely serious, you would probably find it boring. Sarcasm is a form of verbal irony; a sarcastic tone is produced when someone uses heavy-handed verbal irony. Verbal irony occurs when one expresses the opposite of what one actually means. If someone says, "Sure I would *love* to spend the day sweeping, vacuuming, and then mopping the floor, nothing could sound better to me!" that person is almost certainly using irony to convey the fact that cleaning the floors does not sound enjoyable. Here are some additional examples of different tones:

- *Serious tone* from James Baldwin's "Notes of a Native Son," a reflective essay on race: "I learned in New Jersey that to be a Negro meant, precisely, that one was never looked at but was simply at the mercy of the reflexes the color of one's skin caused in other people" (Baldwin, 1955/2007, p. 66).
- *Humorous tone* from David Sedaris's *Me Talk Pretty One Day*: "'I hate you' she said to me one afternoon. 'I really, really hate you.' Call me sensitive, but I couldn't help but take it personally" (Sedaris, 2000).
- *Informational tone* from Todd Pitock's, "In the Forests of the Night," a magazine travel article: "Tigers grow to nine feet long and rule this jungle. . . . According to a display at the Forest Department, the local population is down to 70, a 95 percent decline since 2000" (Pitock, p. 32).

Voice is the style or the character of your writing, and it gives your audience an impression about the writer. Voice is what makes one person's writing distinctive from someone else's. When you listen to music, the voice or style of the band is the reason you can determine which band is the creator of a new song just by hearing the song itself. Word choice, sentence structure, and the level of formality you use in your writing all contribute to your voice. In "Insufficiency of Honesty," Stephen L. Carter establishes a voice of an educated and thorough individual. One way he does this is by defining his terms in his essay:

> When I refer to integrity, I have something very specific in mind. Integrity, as I will use the term, requires three steps: discerning what is right and what is wrong; acting on what you have discerned, even at personal cost; and saying openly that you are acting on your understanding of right and wrong. (Carter, 1996, p. 105)

Carter's voice sounds logical and reasonable because he is carefully defining the term "integrity" and because he has several well-thought-out steps involved in having integrity.

Identifying Appropriate Tone and Voice

It is important to understand the audience for whom you are writing in order to determine the appropriate voice. For instance, you would probably use a more complex sentence structure if you were writing a formal essay for your instructor than if you were writing a love note to your significant other. In a formal essay, you might use the semi-colon or colon to produce more complex sentences that connect thoughts together, but you probably would not use either of these forms of punctuation in a simple love note. That said, in formal essay writing, it is ideal that you vary your sentence structure from sentence to sentence—you should include a mixture of complex sentences, short sentences, and medium-length sentences to convey your thoughts. In all writing, you are aiming for clarity, and sometimes one's thoughts are much clearer in the form of shorter sentences. For any writing assignment you want to make sure that your voice is appropriate for the assignment and the audience for whom you are writing.

When thinking about tone and voice, it is important to remember that our written work is a representation of ourselves to our audience. In fact, tone and voice give the audience a first impression of you as a writer. If your tone uses slang but the assignment is a formal essay, the impression you are giving is that you did not read the assignment carefully enough. Others make judgments about our arguments and thoughts, as well as factors such as our thoroughness and attention to detail, based on our writing. Thus, to achieve your writing purpose and to ensure that your writing is appropriate in your college papers and for your job, you should not only choose your words carefully but also strive to create an impression of yourself that is the best it can be.

Developing the Writer's Voice

We all bring different personalities and our own ideas, experiences, strengths, weaknesses, and intellectual competencies to our writing. We also have our own way of arranging words, our own choices of vocabulary, and our own preferences for sentence structure. These distinctive characteristics of our experiences, personality, and language choices make our writing

GaudiLab/Shutterstock.com

different from the writing of anyone else. When we write, we interact with the audience in our own way, and this interaction helps create and shape the content, style, mood, and tone of our writing.

Voice is a somewhat intangible characteristic of writing. William Strunk, Jr., and E.B. White, authors of a classic guide to writing titled *The Elements of Style* (1959), explain the writer's style as "the sound his words make on paper" (p. 53). Strunk and White believe there is no good explanation of style—that all writers, by the way they use language, reveal their own unique essence. They remind us that writing is a means of communicating with others, and the way that communication works is somewhat mysterious. They ask,

> Who can confidently say what ignites a certain combination of words, causing them to explode in the mind? Who knows why certain notes in music are capable of stirring the listener deeply, though the same notes, slightly rearranged, are impotent? (Strunk & White, 1959, p. 53)

As an example, Strunk and White use a familiar quotation by one of our country's founding fathers, Thomas Paine. As he described the early days of the American Revolutionary War, Paine made the famous statement, "These are the times that try men's souls." Strunk and White suggest we try rewriting this sentence in several different ways. We might say, "Times like these try men's souls," or "These are trying times for men's souls," or even "How trying it is to live in these times!" (Strunk & White, 1959, p. 53).

All these variations on the sentence are grammatically correct and their meaning is clear, but they do not resonate and stay with us like the original sentence. We might say that the original quotation has more of a rhythm than do the variations. However, exactly what gives some words a better rhythm than others and makes some sentences more memorable than others is very difficult to determine. It is the combination of these intangible factors that makes writing an art rather than simply a mechanical process.

If it is so difficult to capture the essence of the writer's art, how can we develop our own style or voice so that our writing is as effective as it can be? Strunk and White provide some guidance here as well. They advise us not to worry about style and to remember that our unique voice is within us. Rather than try to develop our style, they suggest our goal should be to set it free. They recommend we learn all we can about language, the rules of writing, and the characteristics of good writing. As you become proficient in writing, they tell us, your voice will emerge naturally because you yourself will emerge (Strunk & White, 1959). In other words, the more you study the elements of good writing and the more you write, the clearer your voice will become. We can, however, take some steps to "get out of our own way" and enable our unique voice to emerge. Below are some basic rules of thumb about writing to keep in mind as you continue to hone your writing skills.

Be Yourself

While you can learn a great deal from other writers, such as famous authors, family, friends, and classmates, you should not consciously try to imitate or copy others. You may admire techniques that others use and decide to incorporate some them into your own writing, but do so only when they fit naturally for you and can be used as tools to help you develop your own writing style. Remember that you have your own voice that is different from the voices of others. It is your own unique voice that you want to find and develop, not a copy of someone else's.

However, "be yourself" does not mean that you can write anything you want and, as an excuse, say, "Well, I am just being me!" The admonition to be yourself means to be the best "you" that you can be. It means to learn the rules of the writing craft and to use them correctly while also writing naturally and letting your own personality shine through. Your writing creates an impression of who you are. Whether you like it or not, people make judgments about your intelligence, education, manners, habits, and honesty based on your writing. Your objective should be to make that impression as positive as you can.

Be an Ethical Writer

One of the most serious offenses you can commit as a writer is plagiarism—and if you plagiarize, your writing voice will sound completely different from your own. It is important to always remember that when you communicate with others, you have an ethical obligation to be honest and not to take credit for writing that is not your own original work. As discussed in Chapter 1, borrowing someone else's ideas, using a paper you found or buying a paper on the Internet, copying wording from another document, changing a few words of someone else's work without documenting the source, or recycling one of your own papers without permission are all examples of plagiarism.

Many students do not realize that recycling their own papers they submitted for another class is considered plagiarism. As we have discussed, every class has certain learning outcomes, and your written course assignments are intended to help you understand and meet the learning outcomes for that particular class. When you submit a paper for a college course, that paper should be your own individual effort, and it should be an original paper you wrote for that class. If you have written other papers on the same subject in the past, you can use some of the ideas in these earlier papers in your current paper. However, you must consider the previous paper an outside source, just as you would any other source, and document this fact in your new paper. Always keep in mind that you have an ethical responsibility, as a writer, to avoid plagiarism by always giving proper credit to all outside sources you use in your written work.

Spend More Time Revising Than Writing

Many beginning writers spend most of their writing time creating a first draft of their paper and very little time revising and editing that draft. That approach is the exact opposite of the method most experienced writers use when they write. You may not revise and edit your work 39 times, as Earnest Hemingway did with one of his manuscripts; however, all good writing is rewriting. Chapter 4 introduces you to a writing process that provides you with a step-by-step method to follow to create an effective college paper. Every step in the process is important; however, revising and editing usually requires the largest block of time in this process. So, make sure you begin work on your written assignments early in the course week to allow time to refine your initial drafts and create an effective finished product.

Voice and Types of College Writing

One overriding characteristic of good college writing is that it is accurate, concise, and clear. One reason why revising and editing your writing is so important is that it aids you in achieving these important goals. Remember that your objective is to communicate with your reader. If the reader has difficulty reading your paper, following your chain of thought, or grasping your point, your communication will fail. Awkward or difficult sentences, language that is ambiguous, and poorly organized ideas will interfere with your ability to share your ideas with others.

With this in mind, you can and should alter your voice and tailor it to the particular writing assignment. A personal essay may use an emotional voice to great effect, but if a research paper used an emotional voice, it would probably discredit the paper, since research papers are supposed to rely on research and scholarly interpretations. An expository essay may use an objective voice while explaining a subject but then might add a personal voice if the assignment asks the student to include a personal example to help explain their response to the prompt's question. A persuasive essay may use a combination of emotional and logical appeals to the audience, but a research paper generally only uses logic and reasoning to convey an objective voice.

Chapter Summary

The primary purpose of college writing is to share information about a subject, to persuade readers to share your point of view or to take action, or to acquire knowledge through research. College papers generally fall into one of four categories: (1) personal writing, (2) exposition, (3) persuasion and argument, and (4) research papers. At times, the assignment will require a combination of two or more of these types of writing.

Each person approaches writing differently. We make different choices about the words we use and the manner in which we arrange these words. We also interact with readers in different ways. These different characteristics give each of us a unique writing style or voice. As you learn more about the rules and characteristics of good writing and become a more proficient writer, your own unique writing voice will become clearer. Being yourself, remaining an ethical writer, spending more time revising and editing than writing, and remembering to be accurate, concise, and clear when you write all can help you free your inner voice and become the writer you would like to be.

Exercise: Identifying an Essay

For each of the sample essay prompts below, read the assignment and try to determine what kind of essay this assignment is asking for. Circle key words as you read. For each assignment, write four sentences explaining why you think this is the kind of essay you think it is, and what qualities are characteristic of that kind of paper.

Essay 1:

In two to four double-spaced pages (excluding title and reference page), analyze one of the literary works from this week's readings by completing the following:

   a. Describe one of the analytical approaches outlined in Chapter 16, using details from the text to support your interpretations.
   b. Evaluate the meaning of the selected literary work, using the analytical approach you described.

Your paper should be organized around a thesis statement about the selected literary work and the approach you are using to analyze the work. All sources must be properly cited. The paper must include a separate title and reference page, and be formatted to your course's specified documentation style.

Essay 2:

Background: "Adolf Hitler came to power by legal means, appointed by President Paul von Hindenburg on January 30, 1933, according to the constitution of the Weimar Republic. Thereafter, however, he proceeded to dismantle the legal structure of the Weimar system and replace it with an inflexible dictatorship that revolved around his person. . . . The Third Reich was organized as a leader-state, in which Hitler the *Fuhrer* (leader) embodied and expressed the real will of the German people, commanded the supreme loyalty of the nation, and had unlimited authority" (p. 161).

Question: Based on the primary source documents in your text and at least three outside sources, write a three- to four-page paper in response to the following: How did the Nazi Party begin to change the culture of Germany? In your response discuss both:

   a. the Nazi persecution of the Jews
   b. the Nazi policy of territorial expansion.

Essay 3:

Think of a specific location that means something to you, such as the ocean, front porch of a favorite family restaurant, or perhaps a favorite room in your home. In a two- to three- page paper, explain what that location means to you. In describing the location, include detail that impacts three of the five senses—sight, sound, touch, taste, or smell.

Essay 4:

Susan Wolf, in writing about her own father's death, confronts the problems that arise at the end of life, which challenges her to consider her views on assisted suicide. Putting yourself in Wolf's place, consider how you would respond to this tragic and difficult issue. State your own response, arguing for why you think that response is the best available choice. Try to convince someone who might be on the fence why they should agree with your argument. The paper must be at least three pages in length and formatted according to your course's specified documentation style.

Key Terms

appeals to emotion Attempts to create an emotional response in the audience in order to persuade that audience to do or believe something.

expository writing A type of writing that shares information or explains a subject to readers.

objective Based on facts, rather than on personal opinion, about a given topic.

personal writing A type of writing in which the writer states his or her opinion about an issue; documents his or her observations; relates a subject to his or her own life; shares a story; or provides a description of a person, place, object, or event. Personal opinion, narrative essays, and some types of reflection papers fall into this category.

persuasion An attempt to influence others to adopt a certain belief or point of view or to convince them to take some action.

research writing A type of writing that requires the writer to discuss a subject using information gathered from outside sources. These types of assignments may also be called *term papers*, *informative* or *analytical reports*, or *case studies*.

subjective Based on one's own observation, experience, or opinion.

tone The mood the writer conveys about the subject matter. The tone could be skeptical, humorous, serious, or sarcastic, for example.

Selecting a Topic and Prewriting

4

fizkes/Shutterstock.com

Learning Objectives

After reading this chapter, you should be able to do the following:

1. Identify topics that have intellectual merit, as opposed to those that are flippant, frivolous, or alienating.

2. Demonstrate the ability to narrow a topic.

3. Select the best method for you for generating ideas, such as journaling, free writing, or brainstorming.

4. Experiment with different methods for organizing ideas, such as chronologically or logically.

5. Demonstrate your ability to create an outline and a reverse outline.

By writing an outline you really are writing in a way,

because you're creating the structure of what you're going to do.

Once I really know what I'm going to write,

I don't find the actual writing takes all that long.

—Tom Wolfe

From *Essentials of College Writing: Contemporary Applications, 2/E* by Christine M. Connell and Kathy Sole. © 2013 Bridgepoint Education.

This chapter concentrates on selecting and focusing a topic for a college paper and beginning the prewriting process. If you have ever written an outline, you have already done some prewriting. The skills you will learn in this chapter can be applied to personal, expository, persuasive, and research papers, but they are also portable—that is to say, these strategies can help you outside of the classroom experience. Writing is itself a portable skill that will assist you in becoming a better critical thinker, organizer of ideas, and articulator of thoughts and arguments. Effectively selecting a topic and efficiently prewriting are organizational tools that will aid you in synthesizing any information on any subject.

4.1 Selecting a Subject

The first task when beginning a college writing assignment is determining a **subject**, or the general area of interest from which you will select the topic of your paper. Your assignment may provide you with the subject you must write about, or you may be asked to select your own. If you are asked to choose your own subject, it is important to choose one that is appropriate for the assignment and to properly narrow the parameters of your topic, which the following sections will discuss. In either case, remember to use the active reading skills you learned in Chapter 2 to identify key words and phrases and action verbs, and to make certain you clearly understand the purpose and requirements of the assignment.

Understand the Assignment

The subject that you choose to write about should be appropriate for you, the writer. If you have a choice of subject, choose one that interests or excites you. If you are interested in the subject, it will be easier to make it interesting to your readers. It is also fine to choose something you know little about but have always wanted to explore. However, be aware that such a subject will require that you spend additional time researching and referencing sources.

Once you have generated a list of possibilities for your paper, think about which would be most appropriate for the assignment, appeal to you the most, appeal to your audience, and give you the greatest number of possible ideas. One of these subjects will probably be your best choice. For a subject or topic to be considered appropriate, it must fit the purpose of the assignment, the audience, and the writer (you). First, look at the assignment itself and determine the type of writing required. Highlight and underline key words in the assignment to help you understand its focus. Are you being asked to a give personal opinion, explain a task or a process, persuade your readers of something, or argue a point of view? Recall that there are four main types of writing assignments: (1) personal, (2) exposition, (3) persuasion and argument, and (4) research. Each of these assignments requires a different type of topic and a specific pattern of writing, as discussed in Chapter 3. Always look for the page length requirements for any assignment. There is usually a page minimum that is necessary to reach in order to fully answer the prompt's question. Some instructors may also ask that you do not exceed a certain number of pages, so make sure to ask your instructor what his or her specific policy is.

Consider the Audience

In addition to being appropriate for the assignment type, your subject must also be appropriate for your academic audience. Academic writing should be serious and have intellectual merit. Remember that your college assignments are designed to increase your knowledge of serious subjects. Do not be flippant or select silly or frivolous topics. For most assignments, the intended audience consists of your instructor and those in your class, so your tone, or the voice you create, needs to be appropriate for a knowledgeable audience. This means that you write with the assumption that your audience has some knowledge in the subject matter about which you are writing, and therefore you do not need to spend much time at all summarizing the plot or content of a text.

Avoid hot-button topics that may be offensive to your readers. An old adage reminds us to "be careful when talking about sex, politics, and religion at cocktail parties," and this is also good advice for college writing assignments. If you have strong personal beliefs about these subjects, as many of us do, you may alienate some of your readers. Also, unless your assignment is to write a persuasive paper, your goal should not be to convince people to accept your opinion on a topic. For example, it would be appropriate in a personal paper to write about how religion has influenced your life. However, it would not be appropriate to write about why you believe everyone should be religious.

Start With Yourself and What You Know

Begin your search by thinking of subjects on which you have some knowledge. Consider the following questions to generate ideas:

- Do you have any special talents or hobbies?
- What do you do for fun and relaxation?
- What occupies most of your time?
- What experiences have you had that significantly changed your view of the world?
- What is most important to you in your life?

RossHelen/Shutterstock.com

It is usually best to write about a subject of interest to you so that you can convey that interest to your readers. If you are an avid cyclist, you may choose to write about training techniques or bicycle maintenance.

A great number of subjects might be appropriate for an assignment. At this point, do not evaluate the ideas that come to you; just generate a list of possible ideas and write them down as they occur to you. List all ideas, no matter how far fetched they sound. As one of the most prominent chemists of the 20th century, Dr. Linus Pauling once said, "The best way to have a good idea is to have a lot of ideas" (ThinkExist, 2006c). If you have trouble coming up with ideas, try some of the strategies discussed in the feature *Writing in Action: Having Trouble Choosing a Subject?*

> **Writing in Action:** Having Trouble Choosing a Subject?
>
> If you draw a blank trying to find a subject for one of your writing assignments, here are some suggestions that might help you discover subject areas that you can write about:
>
> - *Surf the Web*. Go to your Internet home page and look at the most popular searches, current news, the latest "buzz," or your favorite blogs for possible topics.
> - *Phone a friend*. Bounce ideas off friends or ask them to suggest possible ideas. Sometimes you can spend hours trying to come up with ideas on your own, but a few minutes talking about the assignment with someone else can provide ideas that you would never have thought of on your own.
> - *Do keyword searches*. Use a tool such as Google's AdWords Keyword tool at https://adwords.google.com/o/KeywordTool or the Wordstream Keyword tool at http://www.wordstream.com/keywords/. To try it, put in a term such as "children" or a hobby such as "cycling" and see how many different associated terms appear in the keyword list.
> - *Read articles in an area of interest*. If you subscribe to newspapers and magazines, scan them for possible ideas. Or do an online search for areas of interest and read articles or webpages to learn what others have written about. Don't copy those ideas, of course, but reading other people's ideas will often stimulate ideas of your own or suggest other aspects of a topic that you might write about.
> - *Take a break*. If you are having trouble thinking of topic ideas, take a walk, do the dishes, or listen to music for a few minutes to clear your mind. (Don't procrastinate; be sure to give yourself a time when you must return to your assignment!) When you return to your computer refreshed, you might find that the ideas flow more easily.

4.2 Developing the Topic

Whether you are asked to write a response to an assigned question or to a **topic**—a specific area from a broader subject—of your own choosing, you need to make choices about how you will focus your response. This is more of a concern if you are selecting your own topic. When you have a possible subject to pursue, your next task is to narrow and focus the topic, or subject matter, of your paper. It is generally not enough to just have a topic—one must also have an interpretive question that one wants to explore. This turns a general area of interest into a feasible course of study in a paper. Interpretive questions can be answered in different ways depending on one's analysis of the text or one's research. They are not factual questions that have a set right or wrong answer. A reasonable human being who asks the same interpretive question may develop a different answer.

Narrowing the Topic

One of the most common mistakes students make when choosing a topic is to select one that is too broad and too general. It is much better to choose a narrow topic and deal with it thoroughly than to select a broad topic and treat it in a general or superficial way. For example, suppose your

ChiccoDodiFC/Shutterstock.com

It is always advisable to narrow and focus your topic. A general paper on dogs will be far less interesting to the reader than one focused on the use of German Shepherds in police duty.

assignment is to write a two- to three-page personal narrative paper describing one of your hobbies, and you choose soccer. People can enjoy soccer for many different reasons. Some people like to play competitively, while others are more interested in watching the sport than in playing. As a topic, the term *soccer* is much too broad for a short paper. You will not be able to cover the topic adequately in only a few pages.

You can usually narrow a topic in several different ways. Try to generate a list of alternatives for making the topic of "soccer" more specific. Figure 4.1 illustrates some possibilities. If you think the topic might still be difficult to cover in a short paper, continue to narrow it further, as the figure illustrates.

Figure 4.1: Narrowing the topic

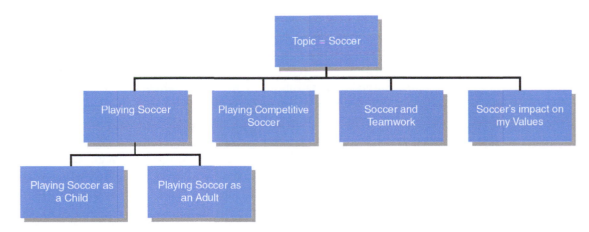

At this point, it is difficult to know whether your topic is narrow enough, or perhaps even too narrow, to the point where you will not have enough information to fill two pages. Do not worry, however, about being too narrow; you can always make adjustments later during the writing process. At this point, the bigger danger is having a topic that is too broad. Once you have generated as many ideas as you can for narrowing the topic, choose the option that is most interesting to you and that you think will best fit the length and purpose of your assignment.

Developing a Focus

After you have selected a subject area and narrowed it to a workable topic, your final task in developing your topic is to create a focus for your paper. Creating a focus will give you a starting point and help you establish a direction for your paper. At this point, merely focus your topic on some aspect of the narrowed topic that you plan to write about.

Let us take our soccer topic as an example. Suppose you decide to narrow the topic to "How soccer has shaped my life" and, in the paper, you want to share information with your readers about how playing soccer for many years has helped to shape your values and character and helped make you the person you are today. Now you have a narrower topic, but you still must focus on some aspect of how soccer has shaped your life that you want to share in your paper.

What is the most important point you want to make to your readers about your soccer experience? Do you want them to know how much fun it is? Is your goal to encourage others to take up the sport? Perhaps your intent is to help readers understand how being a part of a team can change one's perspective. Create a focus for your paper that will narrow your topic even further to some specific goal such as this. Your focus does not have to be a complete sentence, but it should be a single phrase that describes the most important point you want to convey to readers. For instance, your focus for a two- to three-page paper might be to identify the most important way that playing soccer has affected your life. Your specific response to this idea is technically your thesis statement. A **thesis statement** is a response or answer to a question, and in this case, the question would be: "In what ways has playing soccer affected my life?" This essay would create a thesis that answers this question very specifically and that possibly includes the main points the essay as a whole will address. Likewise, each body paragraph should have a topic sentence at the start of the paragraph that will prove one small aspect of the larger thesis statement. In this sense, topic sentences are really mini-arguments or theses articulated at the top of each body paragraph.

In a short paper, you cannot possibly go into detail about all the ways in which soccer affected your life or discuss every game you played. However, you can focus on the one or two experiences you think are the most important and limit your discussion to how those particular experiences affected you.

Be sure to write down the focus you develop so that you can refer to it as you begin to write your paper. Remember, this focus does not meet the requirements for a thesis statement, which should give the reasons why playing soccer has affected your life. The purpose of a focus is merely to help you get started in a clear direction, to help you organize your ideas, and to keep you on track as you write.

As you develop your paper, you may decide that you are more interested in writing about why you decided to take up playing soccer. If you change your mind about the direction of your paper, simply go back and modify your focus. Most writers do not finalize their thesis statement until the last draft of their paper, so think about the focus as merely a starting guideline that is flexible and subject to change. Remember to refer often to the assignment prompt and to continue to make sure that your thesis statement and paper topic are meeting the goals of the assignment.

While you are drafting your paper, you might also find that the topic of playing soccer does not work well. Perhaps you have trouble finding enough to say about the topic or discovering material to support the points you want to make in the paper. Do not be afraid to change your topic if it was a poor choice, but do make this decision early enough that you have sufficient time to write a paper on a different topic. If you begin your writing assignments early in the week they are due, you will have the opportunity to make changes such as this, if necessary.

4.3 Generating Ideas

The first step in the writing process occurs before writing—it occurs when you are using the active reading strategies discussed in Chapter 2. In that chapter you learned that active reading means creating a dialogue with the text.

Ginny Filer/Shutterstock.com

Journaling can be an effective way of generating ideas before writing a paper.

Journaling

Remember that active reading asks you to keep a reading journal of your responses, questions, and insights about the text, and to record these ideas as you are reading. You can do this in a reading journal or through extensively marking up and writing on the text you are reading. Once you are ready to start your paper, you can transform this dialogue into academic writing. Begin by writing informally, sorting through your thoughts as you write. The less you pressure yourself to immediately craft perfect sentences, the better your chances are of avoiding writer's block.

Brainstorming

Brainstorming is any form of writing that allows you to generate ideas. The brainstorming strategy is particularly useful if you do not have clear ideas of what you want to write. The object of the strategy is to get as many ideas as possible down on paper so that you can consider them and find possible directions for your paper—without editing your grammar or your ideas. In brainstorming, quantity of ideas is more important than quality of ideas. You might think of brainstorming as a way of "getting the flow started." You will probably not use all the ideas you generate, but as scientist Dr. Linus Pauling advised, "The way to get good ideas is to get lots of ideas, and throw the bad ones away."

Some companies use a formal brainstorming strategy, with specific rules, as an organizational tool to help produce ideas for solving company problems. However, you can brainstorm without rules by yourself, with one other person, or with a small group of people who are willing to help you. Often, others will think of ideas for your paper that you might not have discovered on your own.

Whether you brainstorm by yourself or with others, use this strategy by just thinking of ideas as quickly as you can and writing them down any way you wish—on a white board, the computer, a large piece of paper, or individual slips of paper. Continue this process until you run out of ideas. Then review the items and eliminate those that you think are unworkable, do not interest you, do not fit well with the other ideas, or will be difficult to cover within the scope of your paper.

Free-Writing

Free-writing is similar in some ways to brainstorming, except free-writing generally involves synthesizing some ideas that have emerged in the brainstorming process. Like brainstorming, free-writing is helpful when you do not have clear ideas of what you want to write about. When you free-write, you begin with a blank piece of paper or a blank document on your computer screen and you can give yourself a time limit, such as 15 or 30 minutes, or a specific length, such as one page of text. Then begin writing and write quickly until you reach that goal. What you write is not as important as the fact that you keep writing until time is up or the page is full. Author Maya Angelou explains free-writing as a method of generating ideas when she states:

> What I try to do is write. I may write for two weeks "the cat sat on the mat, that is that, not a rat." And it might be just the most boring and awful stuff. But I try. When I'm writing, I write . . . . (Nordquist, 2009, p. 1)

The keys to free-writing are to write quickly and not to stop to edit what you write—either for grammar or content. Some people set a timer and turn off their computer monitors to help them resist the temptation to stop, to read what they have written, and to edit. Like Angelou, you may write the same words over and over, create rhymes, or just write, "I am having trouble getting ideas for this paper," repeatedly, until other words begin to come to mind.

Some writers use a free-writing method on the computer screen if they are stuck and other prewriting stages are not working. It may be the case that for one assignment you write a detailed outline and free-write before you start drafting, but for another assignment you simply cannot figure out how you might outline the essay. Different assignments call for different approaches, and it depends on how well you connect with the assignment and have a sense of where to begin.

The value of free-writing is that the words you write often begin to suggest other words, and you then begin to create a draft of your paper. If you have developed a focus for your writing, you might make a copy of that focus and place it next to your computer screen. Then begin typing whatever ideas come to your mind that are related to that focus. Remember to keep writing until you reach the goal you set for yourself. *Writing Samples: Free-Writing Example for the Soccer Paper* shows a section of a free-writing exercise for our soccer paper.

Writing Samples: Free-Writing Example for the Soccer Paper

I've played soccer for years, starting with AYSO when I was about 7. At first, it was just a great way to play outside and meet other girls my age. But continuing to play soccer in middle school and high school, I realized how it was a combination of something incredibly hard and yet so rewarding. I barely had any free time with practices and away games, but I learned so much about making my time count, and I felt so dedicated to my team. Soccer truly has shaped who I am today.

Now that my son Toby is turning 4, I've been thinking more about soccer and how I want him to get him signed up someday soon. It makes me mad when other parents don't see the value of team sports and just give their kids a video game to play instead. In this paper, I would like to persuade people of the benefits you can gain from playing a sport like soccer, as well as how it can shape your character and values in the long-term.

Tree Charts

A tree chart or tree diagram is another strategy for generating ideas and organizing those ideas at the same time. A tree chart resembles an organization chart, and it creates a visual map of your paper. Begin the tree chart with your topic or focus at the top. Then create branches of the tree to show subpoints and additional, smaller branches to illustrate the supporting ideas, detail, or elaboration that support your points and subpoints. Figure 4.2 is an example of a tree chart for the soccer paper.

Figure 4.2: Tree chart for the soccer paper

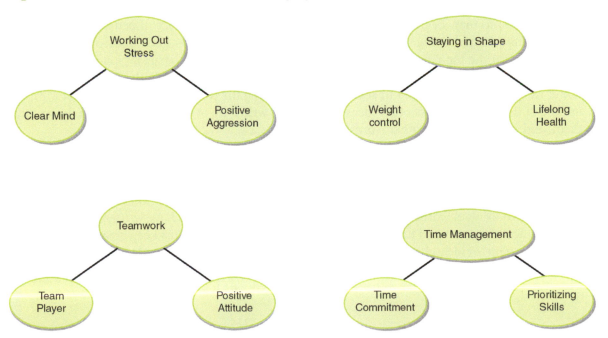

Ask the "Five Ws and an H" Questions

Another strategy for generating ideas is known as Five Ws and an H. These letters stand for the questions *Who*? *What*? *Where*? *When*? *Why*? and *How*? If you are stumped for ideas, particularly when you write about an incident or event, ask yourself the following questions: Who was involved? What happened? Where did it happen? Why did it happen? How did it happen? Answering these questions will often provide you with information to get started on the first draft of your paper.

4.4 Organizing Ideas

After the idea-generating stage, writers should use some method of organizing ideas. Organizing your ideas will help you maintain a clear focus on creating a final paper that presents your arguments and information in a logical way. You might choose to organize ideas visually by using mind mapping, or you might try outlining your ideas. You should try a variety of organizing methods for each assignment, and find a method that works well for you.

Mind Mapping

A **mind map**—also known as a *cluster diagram*, a *bubble diagram*, or a *word web*—is a graphic diagram that illustrates ideas and how they are connected to one another. This strategy uses your creative brain to help you generate ideas. Like brainstorming and free-writing, you can use mind mapping without having clear ideas of what to write about. A mind map organizes ideas, as they come to you, around a key word or idea. Some people like mind mapping because it helps them visualize and classify ideas without worrying about prioritizing and organizing these ideas into an outline.

To create a mind map, begin by making a circle in the middle of a piece of paper or a blank computer document and writing your topic or a key word inside the circle. Then think of ideas or words associated with the topic or key word and write them down as they occur to you. Circle each one and connect it, with a line, to the word in the middle or to another word on the page. For example, a writer can start a mind map of our soccer topic by placing the words *How Soccer Affected Me* in the middle of the page. Then, as other ideas occur to the writer, he or she can write them down, circle them, and connect them to other words on the page.

Remember, there is no right or wrong way to draw a mind map. Just work quickly and record and connect ideas to the topic or key word as soon as you think of them, without judging them as good or bad. At first, the ideas may seem random and disconnected from one another. However, you will soon begin to think of words that are associated with other words you have written. When this happens, connect the new word to one of the previous words you wrote. Just keep creating connections until you run out of ideas. If an idea occurs to you that is relevant but does not seem to fit with other words you have written, draw another line of association from the word in the center of the page. View the mind map in Figure 4.3 that was created to generate ideas for the soccer paper.

Figure 4.3: Mind map

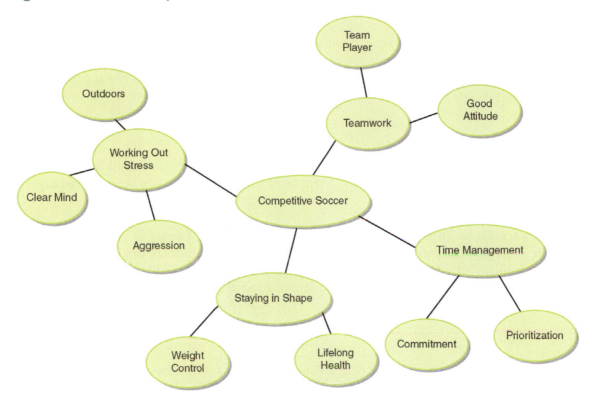

If you run out of ideas while you are creating your mind map, go back to your topic or key word in the center of the page and think of a new direction. Or ask yourself questions such as "What if I wrote about . . . ?" or "What else could I include in the paper?" Sometimes you will have very short word associations or branches from your topic; at other times, the words you write will lead to many other words, and you have a strong thread of ideas that could create a focus for your paper. You might even want to use one of the many free or proprietary software programs on the market today to help you create your mind map. Go online and search for "mind-mapping software" and check out some of the available programs such as Bubble.us, XMind, or FreeMind. The widely used software Inspiration even allows you to automatically turn your mind map into an outline.

Mind-mapping applications are also available for the iPhone and iPod Touch. ThinkDigits 2.0, for example, is a combination of mind-mapping software and a calculator; Headspace provides 3D visual mapping; and iThoughts has functionality that allows you to cut, copy, paste, and merge topics.

Outlining

You might also consider outlining before you start writing the first paragraph of any paper. **Outlining** is a method of organization that allows you to sort out your thoughts and to notice what points seem to be the most significant. Sometimes, a paper works well following a chronological order, but more often than not, a paper should follow some other organizational structure. This may include tracing and explaining the steps of an argument you read, countering a position, or even completely reordering the sequence of events you read so that they are presented in a manner of increasingly strengthening your argument. You might order your body paragraphs according to the development of a central theme in the text, and this may not happen in chronological order in the text.

Your outline can be an informal scratch outline, or a formal, detailed outline. Try to develop some type of outline when you think you have finished your prewriting process but before you start drafting your paper. This will help you organize your paper and think through the best possible order for your main points.

Scratch Outlines

A **scratch outline** is a rough outline that lists the ideas in the order you intend to discuss them. When you begin the outline, your creative brain takes charge and helps you generate and organize ideas.

To create a scratch outline, first list your ideas as described earlier. Then, edit your list and remove the ideas you think are unworkable, do not fit with the other ideas, or are too broad to include in your paper. Finally, organize the remaining items on your list into the order you think you would like to discuss them in the paper. *Writing Samples: Ideas for the Soccer Paper* shows an example of a scratch outline for the soccer paper.

Writing Samples: Ideas for the Soccer Paper

Focus: To persuade the reader that competitive soccer is not just a hobby, but an activity that can influence his or her character and values.

Long practices
Committing to workouts and game schedules
Working with teammates who rely on you
Juggling soccer, school, work, and family
Traveling for soccer games
Staying in shape
Exercising for fun
Taking care of uniform and equipment
Working out stress
Spending time outside
Winning and losing
Keeping a positive attitude
Being a team player

Formal Outlines

A **formal outline** is created the same way as a scratch outline; however, you create a more structured outline by numbering your ideas and detailing the pieces of evidence you will use and in which section of the paper they will appear. When you outline, always reread your outline and ask yourself if your main points build on each other. Many great papers begin the first body paragraph by discussing the conclusion of the text they have read. Imagine if you were reading a paper someone wrote on *Antigone* and the writer did not mention until the very last paragraph that Antigone dies! If you decide to create a formal outline (or if a formal outline is required for your assignment), review *Writing in Action: Producing a Formal Outline* for information on how to create this type of outline.

Writing in Action: Producing a Formal Outline

A formal outline can be an effective way to generate and organize ideas for your college papers. The formal outline not only indicates the ideas that will be discussed in the paper and the order in which the ideas will be presented but also shows the relationship between those ideas.

In a formal outline, the main sections of your paper, or the main points in the body of the paper, are listed first. Then these main ideas are subdivided again and again, into subpoints, which are the facts and information that support that main idea. Each breakdown, or level, of points is more specific and more detailed than the level above it. Here are some basic rules for outlining.

Rules for Outlining

1. Outline beginning with Roman numerals for the main points in the paper and then alternate between numbers and letters as you subdivide these main points into more detailed subpoints.
2. Some people create an outline for the entire paper, showing the introduction, body, and conclusion of the paper, to make sure they do not forget any of the required elements. Others outline only the body of the paper, showing only the main points and the supporting ideas. To make sure your paper is complete, you should outline the entire paper.
3. Points can continue to be subdivided to the level of detail needed. Most outlines are subdivided to only the third level (1, 2, etc.) or the fourth level (a, b, etc.), as shown in the outline template below.
4. When you divide something (think of a pie, an apple, or a candy bar), you always get at least two pieces. Therefore, in an outline, remember that you should never have an A without a B, a 1 without a 2, and so on. If you have only one point to make about a certain issue in your outline, work that point into the issue itself in order not to create a subdivision.
5. Each main point and subdivision should contain a single idea, and all subpoints should be related to or support the points above them.
6. All points at the same level must be expressed the same way throughout the outline: either as all complete sentences, all phrases, or all single words. You can have a variety of different expressions, as long as all points at the same level in the outline are expressed similarly. For example, if Roman numeral I, subpoint A is a complete sentence, then all A, B, C (etc.) subpoints in Roman numerals I, II, and III must be complete sentences.
7. Headings I, II, III (etc.) must be approximately balanced. In other words, you should have approximately the same amount of material under each of these main points.

Creating the Outline

Begin your outline by writing your topic at the top of a blank page. Then write the Roman numerals I, II, and III, spread apart down the left side of the page.

1. *Outlining the entire paper.* If you want to outline your entire paper, write the words "Introduction," "Body," and "Conclusion" next to each Roman numeral. Then, write A, B, C (etc.) indented under each Roman numeral.

(continued)

Writing in Action: Producing a Formal Outline *(continued)*

Next to the capital letters under "I. Introduction," list the elements of a good introduction. Next to each element, write what you plan to say about each of these elements. Next to the capital letters under "II. Body," list the main points you plan to make in the body of your paper. Finally, next to Roman numeral "III. Conclusion," list the elements of a good conclusion and what you will include for each of the conclusion elements.

Once you have finished completing the top two levels of your outline, go back to the capital letters A, B, C (etc.) and, under each one of these letters in section II, write the statements you will make to support, explain, elaborate, or provide more detail about each of those main points.

2. *Outlining only the body of the paper.* If you plan to outline only the body of your paper, write each main body point next to Roman numerals I, II, III (etc.). You should have between two and six main points for your paper, regardless of length. Long papers do not have more main points than short papers; longer papers simply have more supporting information and more explanation about each main point.

Outline Template

The template below offers a method of organization that writers can use for essentially any thesis-driven paper. Whenever you are unsure about how to outline your ideas, you can refer to the model below:

I. Introduction
   A. Title of work and authors the paper will discuss
   B. Information or context that sets the stage for answering the paper prompt
   C. A tentative thesis statement
II. Body Paragraph (Note: you will likely have several body paragraphs that follow the format suggested here. There is no magical number of paragraphs necessary for papers; just write enough body paragraphs with main ideas to fully respond to the essay prompt.)
   A. Topic sentence should make an argument or **claim** and state what you will prove in this paragraph. It should be directly related to the thesis statement and should only try to prove one small part of the thesis statement.
   B. An example with direct citation from the text. Introduce citations before giving the quote and always integrate citations into your own sentences. A citation can never be a sentence by itself—it must include your language in order to function properly within a paper.
   C. An explanation that describes how the evidence supports the claim you are making in this paragraph. You should not simply summarize an example or piece of evidence: Instead, you should directly explain how the example offered supports the main claim of that paragraph. Another example that supports your argument.
   D. Another explanation.
   E. (Note: A body paragraph may have several more pieces of evidence and the explanations and analysis that go along with them).
   F. Concluding sentences that explain how these pieces of evidence relate to and build on one another.
III. Conclusion
   A. Should explain what the evidence ultimately suggests. Reflect on the significance of the evidence you have cited and the connections you have made in each paragraph. Try to connect these paragraphs by answering a broader question called the "So what?" question, which asks you to state why this topic is important to discuss.

Writing down main ideas following the basic guidance of an outline structure will help you reflect on how your ideas are developing. See *Writing Samples: Formal Outline for the Soccer Paper* for a more concrete example of how to outline an essay.

Writing Samples: Formal Outline for the Soccer Paper

I. Introduction
   A. Hook: If you think that physical sports such as soccer are simply about pursing a hobby or burning calories, this paper should help you to reconsider the ways that playing soccer can impact your life.
   B. Purpose and Topic: Knowing how sports like soccer can help you grow as a person and enrich your life is very important.
   C. Thesis Statement: Competitive soccer can not only help you work out your stress and stay in shape, but it can also teach you key values such as teamwork and time management that translate to other aspects of your life and work.
   D. Preview: This paper will discuss the ways that soccer can influence a person's character and values.

II. Body
   A. Working Out Stress
      1. Spending time outside, engaged in physical activity, can help clear your mind and ease stress from the day.
      2. Through playing soccer, you can train yourself to work out stress and aggression in positive ways.
   B. Staying in Shape
      1. Playing a sport like soccer regularly will help keep your weight in check.
      2. Playing soccer will promote overall lifelong health, such as heart health and blood pressure.
   C. Teamwork
      1. Soccer can teach you how to be a true team player, with others relying on you to do your part for the team.
      2. Keeping a positive attitude is essential to a team's happiness and success.
   D. Time Management
      1. Workout and game schedules require long-term commitment, in addition to showing up on time.
      2. Learning to juggle soccer with other obligations—such as school, work, and family—will help you prioritize responsibilities.

III. Conclusion
   A. Signal: Now that I have shared the various ways that playing competitive soccer can enrich your life experiences and impact your character, I hope that you look at the value of team sports with new eyes.
   B. Summary: Before you dismiss team sports as no more than a simple "hobby," consider the ways in which a sport like soccer can influence your stress levels, physical fitness, teamwork values, and time management skills.
   C. Final Statement: Then you can choose to sign up for a fun-filled activity that will make you focused, fit, and dedicated, and maybe rack up some great wins along the way.

Reverse Outlining

Another approach is to create what is called a **reverse outline**, or a type of outline that is written after an essay has been drafted. Free-write your ideas first, brainstorm your connections between pieces of text, draft your essay, and then read the essay and record the outline of the draft. This can be very revealing because it will show you whether or not you had main points, evidence, and **warrants**, or explanations of how the evidence you have cited supports your claims, in each body paragraph. Look at your outline and ask yourself whether the main points in the body paragraphs support the thesis statement. Another question to ask is whether the main points develop your thesis sufficiently—does one point build on another? Do they demonstrate the arc of your thesis progressively? If you have a main point that you think is weaker, you likely want to place that toward the beginning of the essay in the first or second body paragraph. The last body paragraph should be the culmination of the preceding paragraphs and should demonstrate a sophisticated understanding of the assignment.

4.5 Prewriting: Putting It All Together

Below is an outline used by the writer to organize her thoughts before drafting the essay as well as a sample portion of the soccer paper. The outline should indicate the main ideas the writer wants to convey. Good outlines use descriptive words and phrases and indicate a level of detailed thought. Keep in mind that before the student could write an outline, the student had to go through the stage of ideas generation first, either with free-writing or brainstorming, or both. And prior to outlining, the student may have also used mind mapping and idea **clustering** (grouping ideas together and branching them off into separate bubbles) as a first step in the organization process after the ideas generation stage.

Writing Sample: Soccer Paper Outline

I. What is the most fulfilling part about playing competitive soccer?
   A. Bonding with teammates
   B. Learning how to be a team player
II. What things do you remember about playing soccer as a child?
   A. Learning the rules
   B. Learning to work with others to accomplish goals
III. What things do you remember about playing soccer later in life?
   A. Learning what it means to work hard
   B. Learning what it means to work as a team
   C. Making a commitment to playing on a team
IV. What are your greatest achievements so far?
   A. Applying what I learned playing soccer to being a parent
   B. A lifelong path to fitness and wellness
   C. Making new friends through soccer
   D. Staying disciplined and focused

After creating this outline, the student likely was able to move to the drafting stage. As you read the excerpt below (consisting of the introduction and first body paragraph), note how it is has followed the first part of the outline and how its ideas are consistently organized.

mimagephotography/Shutterstock.com

Writing Sample: Excerpt from Sample Soccer Essay

What is the most fulfilling part about playing competitive soccer? Perhaps you guessed winning trophies, adrenaline highs, or staying in great shape. But in my experience, bonding with teammates and learning how to be a true team player top the list. Thinking back on my many years as a soccer player, I have realized how important the game of soccer has been in developing my greatest friendships, along with a positive attitude toward teamwork that has in turn influenced other aspects of my life. Playing soccer has caused me to grow as a person, influencing my values and the outlook on life I have today.

For one thing, soccer has helped me to make friendships that have lasted throughout the stages of my life. I remember loving soccer from day one, even if I barely understood the concept of the game. When I was just 6 years old, my mother signed me up for a local AYSO team (American Youth Soccer Organization) that played around the corner from our church. I had always been a spunky and energetic little girl, preferring to climb trees rather than play with Barbie dolls, but soccer brought out something new in me. Suddenly, I had to learn the rules of the game, and to learn how to work with a bunch of other girls that I just met. In that first year or two, it was all about being together with my teammates, kicking around the small black-and-white ball, wondering what we would eat for snack time, and pulling up grass with our fingers. Luckily, a couple of those girls grew into two of my best friends. Now that we are starting our own families, we can think back on those days and get excited about signing up our own children for soccer one day.

Although the essay is a personal narrative, regardless of the writing assignment, as a writer you want to create interest in your subject and you usually will want to convey some form of a thesis or argument about the subject.

Chapter Summary

This chapter has discussed the process of selecting a suitable topic to pursue over the course of a paper, including how to narrow your topic and establish a focus for your paper. Recall that, when starting an assignment, it is important to choose a subject that is appropriate for you, the writer. You will be better able to create interest in your paper for the reader if you are interested in the subject while writing. Once you have selected your subject, you should choose a topic from within that subject area on which to focus your paper. When choosing a topic, it is a good idea to choose one that is narrow so you can address it thoroughly in your paper.

After narrowing your topic and developing a focus, the next step in prewriting is to generate ideas. There are methods of generating ideas that include brainstorming and free-writing. After the ideas generation stage, a writer's ideas need organization, and that can be done through mind mapping, clustering, outlining, and reverse outlining. You may not use each one of these methods for an essay, but you will likely benefit from using a combination of them. These steps should help you feel prepared to take on the next step of the writing process, structuring and developing a paper, which will be covered in Chapter 5. Remember, a polished final draft of an essay does not simply fall from the sky—it takes prewriting, thinking, and revision stages to arrive at the strongest representation of your response to a writing prompt.

Key Terms

claim A statement that asserts an argument about a subject, text, or topic.

clustering A method of brainstorming that involves grouping ideas together and branching them off into separate bubbles that contain different ideas.

formal outline A type of outline that may contain numbers or letters to order an essay's main points. It usually also includes the evidence or quotes the paper will use for each body paragraph.

free-writing An informal method of writing out ideas to get some thoughts on paper without worrying about issues of grammar, mechanics, and structure.

mind map A visual map of ideas for a paper.

outlining A process of arranging ideas into an intended organization for a paper. It usually contains a formal letter and number style, and specific information such as a tentative thesis statement.

reverse outline A type of outline that is written after an essay has been drafted.

scratch outline A list of ideas that will be covered in an essay. A scratch outline is usually written prior to a formal outline, but in some cases a writer may feel ready to skip the scratch outline.

subject The general area of interest from which the topic of a paper is selected.

thesis statement A sentence that makes an arguable claim that the paper will support and develop over the course of the paper.

topic A specific area of focus taken from a broader subject.

warrants Explanations of how the evidence cited in a paper supports the paper's claims; in essence, it analyzes the evidence and interprets it.

Structuring and Developing a Paper

frankie's/Shutterstock.com

Learning Objectives

After reading this chapter, you should be able to do the following:

1. Execute a well-structured introduction to a college essay.

2. Organize the body of a college essay.

3. Implement writing tools to create a functional conclusion.

4. Identify paper types and their corresponding structures.

5. Demonstrate your understanding of the writing process.

Sometimes [writing's] like driving through fog. You can't really see where you're going. You have just enough of the road in front of you to know that you're probably still on the road, and if you drive slowly and keep your headlamps lowered you'll still get where you were going. . .

And sometimes you come out of the fog into clarity, and you can see just what you're doing and where you're going, and you couldn't see or know any of that five minutes before.

—Neil Gaiman

This chapter offers specific guidelines for developing and structuring an essay's introduction, body paragraphs, and conclusion. The purpose of an introduction is not only to capture the reader's interest but also to discuss the purpose and significance of the topic explored in the paper. This chapter discusses different methods for developing the structure of your paper, from developing an attention-grabbing introduction through writing a strong conclusion. The end of the chapter also offers a discussion of how to structure the different types of paper assignments you will encounter in your academic career. Regardless of the type of paper you are writing, however, you should always consider the "Five Cs of Academic Writing," which are the five primary overarching goals of a college paper. When you submit your final paper, it should be:

1. Complete
2. Coherent
3. Clear
4. Concise
5. Correct.

5.1 The Introduction

We will discuss the introduction of the paper first because it is the beginning of the paper. However, just because it is read first does not mean that you will write it first. When we work our way from the topic to the focus, the thesis, the main ideas, and the paper itself, our ideas evolve and change. You may not know exactly what you plan to say until you have written the first draft of the paper. The **introduction** begins your discussion of the topic and sets the stage for the rest of the paper. A good introduction accomplishes four primary goals. It

1. captures the readers' attention and interests them in reading more;
2. reveals the purpose of the paper and the topic;
3. presents the thesis statement; and
4. previews the main points covered in the body of the paper.

Visualize the ideas in your introduction as an inverted triangle—you should begin with a broad introduction to the subject and offer context, but as your introduction proceeds, it should become more specific and detail the point of the paper. For instance, with the soccer topic we examined in Chapter 4, the writer began by selecting the broad subject area, "Soccer" (Figure 5.1, Part A). She narrowed that broad area to the more limited topic, "How soccer has shaped my life," and created a focus (Figure 5.1, Part B). After you've narrowed the focus of your paper and come up with a hook, you can begin turning those elements into a strong introduction by adhering to the following principles.

Figure 5.1: Visualizing your introduction

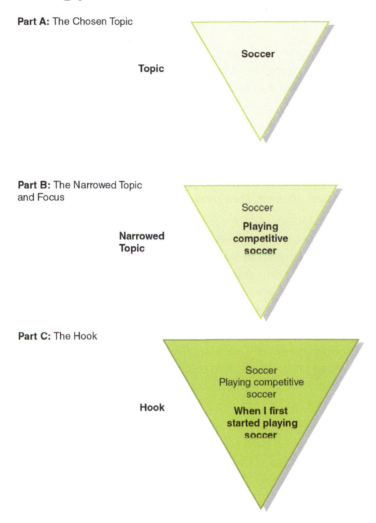

Capture the Reader's Attention

The first few sentences of a paper are sometimes called the **hook** because these initial sentences should capture readers' attention and interest them enough that they want to keep reading. *Writing in Action: Strategies for Hooking the Reader* lists some strategies that you might use to hook your readers and some examples of opening sentences for our soccer paper that use each of these strategies. Regardless of which strategy you choose, make sure that your opening sentences are brief and to the point. Also remember that you must tie the opening sentences to your topic and to your thesis statement later in your introduction.

Writing in Action: Strategies for Hooking the Reader

1. Make a statement that arouses readers' curiosity.
   Example: There was a roaring sound in my ears, and the crowd around me was a blur of faces. A teammate yelled my name as my foot connected with the ball, sending it hurtling towards the goal just in time.

2. Use a relevant quotation. (*Note*: Remember to *cite* the source of the quotation.)
   Example: Bill Shankly, Liverpool manager, was once quoted as saying, "Some people believe football is a matter of life and death. I'm very disappointed with that attitude. I can assure you it is much, much more important than that" (SoccerNews Web Site, 2010, para 2). Having played soccer for over 10 years, I can certainly say that soccer has shaped my life in unforgettable ways.

3. Tell a brief story or share a short anecdote. (*Note*: Your story should be true; if it is not, to be ethical you must tell the reader at some point in the paper that it was an imaginary tale.)
   Example 1: As far back as I can remember, I have been a tomboy at heart. My early years were spent climbing trees, catching frogs, and building forts with my younger brothers. However, my love of team sports did not begin until I played in my first soccer game.

   Example 2: Imagine a newspaper headline that reads, "Senior girls pull off huge win in California State soccer championship!" Such a headline can become real only if you dedicate yourself to years of late-night practices, develop complete trust in your teammates, and embrace the adrenaline rush that comes with playing competitive soccer.

4. Make an intriguing, startling, or controversial statement that you intend to prove or disprove later.
   Example: Soccer is just a hobby. It's not something that you can build your life around. Young athletes might hear sayings like these often, but they are not necessarily true. The time commitment, friendships, and physical strength required by competitive soccer can travel with you wherever you go.

5. Present a problem or dilemma.
   Example: You want to get in shape, but you don't want to hang out in the gym with only your iPod for company. Getting involved in a team sport like soccer could be the answer for both your fitness plan and your social life.

6. Explain a concept important to your topic.
   Example: The World Cup is an international soccer championship that is played every four years. While only national teams can compete in the games, every true soccer fan follows this event, which is essentially the "Olympic games" of the soccer world.

7. Ask a question and immediately answer it.
   Example: What is the most fulfilling part about playing competitive soccer? Perhaps you guessed winning trophies, adrenaline highs, or staying in great shape. But in my experience, bonding with teammates and learning how to be a true team player tops the list.

8. Ask a question that you will answer later in the paper.
   Example: What's so fulfilling about playing a competitive sport like soccer? Read on to hear how what started out as a simple hobby has shaped me into the person I am today.

(continued)

Writing in Action: Strategies for Hooking the Reader *(continued)*

9. Ask a **rhetorical question** (one in which an answer is not expected because it is assumed to be obvious).
   Example: How would you like to be in peak physical fitness, have over a dozen amazing friends whom you get to see every week, and spend your free time playing outside in the sun? All this can be yours if you join a competitive soccer team.

10. Present an opinion contrary to yours and then refute it.
    Example: I once overheard a friend say that she would rather play video games than break a sweat any day. Don't fall into this trap! While video games can be fun, breaking a sweat with a sport like competitive soccer can give you much greater rewards in the long term than an online high-score.

11. Present a surprising statistic. (*Note*: Make sure that it is accurate and cite your source.)
    Example: Some 6,000 youth soccer clubs are part of U.S. Youth Soccer, the organization that supports 3.2 million young soccer players all across the United States (SoccerNation Web Site, 2012).

12. Provide interesting historical background.
    Example: The history of contemporary soccer spans more than 100 years. It all began when the Football Association of England was formed in 1863 (FIFA Web Site, 2013).

13. Create a visual image or appeal to the readers' senses with your words.
    Example: Imagine yourself kicking a game-winning ball into the opposing team's goal in the final moments of the match. As the ball clears the net, your euphoric teammates surround you and the stadium erupts in cheers.

14. Use dialogue to create interest.
    Example: "This is it, ladies," the team captain announced, her voice brimming with a mixture of determination and excitement. "The big match we've all been working for all season has arrived." (*Note*: Make sure that you explain this dialogue later in the paper.)

As you can see from *Writing in Action: Strategies for Hooking the Reader*, there are many different options for beginning a paper. Choose an opening that seems natural and appealing and that you believe is appropriate for your audience, your topic, and the assignment. Your overall goal is to have a strong, forceful opening. Now that you know some tips about how to compose your hook, here are some warnings on what is not very effective:

- Do *not* bore your readers with a long story that is only slightly or tangentially related to the assignment.
- Do *not* begin by announcing your intentions: "The purpose of this paper is . . . ," "In this paper, I will show . . . ," or "The topic of this paper is . . . ." Announcing your purpose later in the introduction with a statement such as, "In this paper, I intend to . . ." is fine. In fact, as we discuss in the next section, you must reveal the purpose and topic of your paper at some point in your introduction. However, do not start your paper with that information. Construct a strong hook first.

- Do *not* begin with vague generalities such as "From the dawn of time . . ." or "When I was growing up . . . ." Try to be more specific and more creative.
- Do *not* use an opening strategy just for effect. In other words, do not make a startling statement just because it is startling and will get attention. Your opening statements must tie into your topic and the purpose of your paper in some way, even if that tie-in is not revealed until much later in the paper.
- Do *not* begin with the definition of a term, especially from a dictionary. Avoid defining terms in the introduction. If you think it is necessary to define a term, do so in a body paragraph, and define the term according to how the text you are writing about uses that term (rather than a dictionary definition).

Reveal the Paper's Purpose and the Topic

The introduction sets the stage for the rest of the paper and prepares readers for what you will cover later in the body of the paper. A common way to think about the function of the introduction is that it "tells readers what you will tell them." When you introduce the purpose of your paper and the topic, simply explain clearly to your readers what the paper will be about. It is not wrong to state "The purpose of this paper is . . ."; however, it is better to be a bit more creative and weave the purpose and the topic into the introduction in another way.

Suppose you have been asked to write a personal essay. Let us use one of our opening strategies for the soccer paper from Chapter 4 to illustrate how you might continue after the opening statement to reveal the purpose of the paper and the topic:

> When I joined the soccer team in middle school, I never imagined how much soccer would affect my life. Years later, I can easily see how playing soccer helped to shape my values and character and helped make me the person I am today.

Crafting the Thesis Statement

When you chose your topic, you created a focus for your paper. As you develop your paper, you must make that focus more specific and turn it into a thesis statement. The thesis statement is a single sentence that makes an assertion, or a specific statement, about your topic, and it is an argument that is based on your interpretation. You might think of the thesis statement as a recap or brief summary of the scope of your paper. Imagine if someone said to you, "I don't have time to read your paper. Tell me the main idea or the bottom line in 25 words or less." Your thesis is a single sentence that responds to that request.

The Controlling Idea

Think of the thesis statement as the unifying force of your paper. It helps direct your thinking about the topic in a specific direction, and it helps control the paper and keeps you on track as you write. In fact, the thesis is sometimes referred to as the controlling idea. Do not confuse your topic with your thesis. The topic is the subject of your paper; the thesis is an assertion you make about the topic—a specific statement about the topic that you intend to elaborate on and support. This assertion is usually made in the introduction of the paper, and is typically the last sentence or two of the paragraph. Please bear in mind that you should ask your instructor if he or she would prefer a one-sentence or two-sentence thesis statement. Some assignments, if they are particularly complex, may require a two-sentence thesis.

Your thesis should be an explicit statement about what you intend to argue over the course of the paper. Most thesis statements for expository, argument, and research papers also include the main points the paper aims to cover. For most assignments, a thesis statement with main points is ideal because the point of the thesis is to communicate the architecture of your paper (however, keep in mind that in any kind of personal essay, you may not need to include your main points—always ask your instructor if you are unsure about what kind of thesis the assignment is asking for). You can think of the thesis as a kind of road map for your paper—just by reading the thesis, the reader should have a clear sense of what you will argue and why. A thesis statement may even include an aspect of the opposing viewpoint in order to show that you have considered it. You could formulate the sentence along these lines: "Although it may seem that Proposition X is eco-friendly, it is not in regards to X, Y, and Z points." Taking into consideration the opposition shows that you are fair-minded and will help you strengthen your argument.

XiXinXing/Shutterstock.com

It can be helpful to think of your introduction as a road map, telling your readers where you plan to take them.

One effective way to develop a thesis statement is to form a question and then answer it. For example, after reading a novel in which a fire occurs, you may wonder: "Is the use of fire as a theme in this novel more destructive or creative?" A thesis statement is an answer to an interpretive question. An answer, or tentative thesis statement, could read: "Though the use of fire is typically considered destructive, in this novel it is a creative source or regeneration." This thesis offers a possible answer to the question. After writing the body paragraphs, one could return to the thesis and elaborate with clear main points.

You might also think of your paper as a discussion you are having with your readers about an issue. In your thesis statement, you take a stand on this issue. The thesis statement tells readers what the discussion will be about and informs them of your position on the subject. If your readers remember nothing else about your paper, you want to make sure that they remember the thesis. So, you must make it clear and specific.

Remember that your thesis statement is an assertion that is more specific than your focus and is the major idea that you want to convey to readers. For example, suppose you are writing a paper on small businesses, and you have one major idea: the use of independent contractors by small businesses. You might ask this question: "What is the relationship between independent contractors and small business hiring practices?" When you answer the question, your thesis statement might read as follows: "The use of independent contractors is the most important change in hiring practices for small businesses in this century." This sentence is your thesis. Remember that your topic or your focus may change as you write your paper. If so, make sure to go back and change your thesis statement as well so that it reflects exactly what you cover in the paper.

Elements of a Strong Thesis

Let us look at the elements of a strong thesis. An effective thesis

- expresses one major idea;
- names the topic and asserts something specific about it;
- is more specific than the focus that you developed earlier;
- summarizes the main points in the body of the paper;
- is an interpretation about which reasonable people might disagree;
- states your position on or opinion about the issue;
- includes a rationale that explains why the argument you plan to make is significant. For instance, if you say "In Martin Luther King's 'Letter from Birmingham Jail,' he uses many rhetorical devices" you have not yet stated an argument. You would have to say something about these rhetorical devices such as: "he uses logos, an appeal to reasoning, in order to argue that only unreasonable individuals would disagree with him." This revision includes a "so what?"

On the other hand, a thesis statement is *not* a question—think of a thesis as your answer to a question:

- Poor thesis statement: Why do philosophers disagree on what happiness is?
- Strong thesis statement: Happiness is not an easily defined state of being; thus, many philosophers disagree on what happiness is.

A thesis statement is *not* a statement of fact:

- *Poor thesis statement:* The philosopher Socrates thought that justice was important.
- *Strong thesis statement:* In *The Republic*, Socrates implies that happiness is the result of living a just life.

A thesis statement is *not* an announcement:

- *Poor thesis statement:* My thesis statement is about the pros and cons of affirmative action.
- *Strong thesis statement:* Affirmative action is a method of promoting equality in light of past injustices, and it can be an effective and fair part of the college admissions process if two potential candidates are equally qualified.

If you are writing an expository or an argument paper, a thesis statement is *not* a statement about you:

- *Poor thesis statement:* I agree with Socrates that justice is important, so he must be correct about it.
- *Strong thesis statement:* Justice, as Socrates suggests, allows one to not only attain happiness but also to live according to the important human ability to use reason.

If, on the other hand, you have a personal essay to write, it is expected that you use the first person "I." It may even be the case that the focus of the paper should be your opinion on a particular subject (rather than your interpretation, which means a careful analysis of a text).

To make sure that you have an effective thesis statement, check it against the checklist in *Writing in Action: Checklist for an Effective Thesis Statement*. If your thesis statement does not meet all these criteria, keep working on it until you can check all boxes in the checklist.

Writing in Action: Checklist for an Effective Thesis Statement

When you have written the thesis statement for your paper, check it against the list below to make sure it meets all the requirements for an effective thesis.

My thesis statement:

- is one complete sentence, not a sentence fragment or a question.
- expresses one major idea.
- names the topic and asserts something specific about it.
- is more specific than the focus statement developed earlier.
- summarizes the main points made in the body of the paper.
- is an issue about which reasonable people might disagree.
- states my position on or opinion about the issue.

Preview the Main Points of the Paper

If you have a thesis statement that outlines each of the main points you plan to cover, as in the case of the four main points in our soccer paper thesis, you already have a clear preview. Your thesis statement has done "double duty" by serving as both a thesis and a preview.

If the main points you plan to cover in the body of your paper are not incorporated into the thesis statement, you must construct another sentence or two that becomes the preview and informs your readers of what you intend to cover in the paper. For example, in our small business paper, the thesis statement was the following: "The use of independent contractors is the most important change in hiring practices for small businesses in this century." Now you must create a preview to prepare readers for what they will find in the paper. Do you intend to give readers historical information about hiring practices and how they have evolved to those of today, or do you want to discuss the benefits of using independent contractors or the duties they can perform? Your preview should provide readers with a road map for the rest of the paper that follows.

Setting Reader Expectations

Remember that you must always consider the needs of your audience when you write. If you are presenting a topic that might be new to your readers, for example, you might want to give background information to help them understand the topic. If you are making suggestions or recommendations, you might anticipate that your audience may question what qualifies you to make those recommendations. Thus, you may want to present your personal experiences, background, or educational qualifications to lend credibility to your statements. Your essay will also demonstrate your credibility if you use a respectful tone toward other writers. Do not forget to consider the writing situation and the rhetorical context when you write.

Remember that the introduction sets the stage for what you are trying to accomplish. To complete the introduction, you may want to elaborate on your thesis statement to prepare the audience for what they will read or what you will or will not cover in the paper. *Writing Samples: Sample Soccer Paper Introduction* illustrates a complete introduction for the soccer paper, with all elements of the introduction numbered and labeled in Figure 5.2.

Writing Samples: Sample Soccer Paper Introduction

Soccer is just a hobby. It's not something that you can build your life around. Young athletes might hear sayings like these often, but they are not necessarily true. The time commitment, friendships, and physical strength required by competitive soccer can travel with you wherever you go.[1] Thinking back on my many years playing competitive soccer, I have realized how important the game of soccer has been in developing my values and the person I am today. If you think that physical sports such as soccer are simply about pursuing a hobby or burning calories, this paper should help you to reconsider the ways that playing soccer can impact your life.[2] Competitive soccer has not only helped me work out my stress and stay in shape, but it has also taught me key values such as teamwork and time management that translate to other aspects of my life and work.[3]

Figure 5.2: Components of the introduction

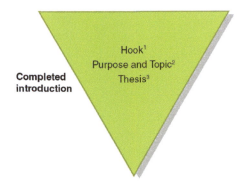

It is possible that you may not create your final thesis statement until very late in the writing process. As you write, you will probably find that you get new ideas, and you may change direction more than once before you finalize your paper. Likewise, discussing your ideas with your instructor and classmates is also an important method for strengthening your ideas. These changes are all part of the writing process. Writing is often a process of ongoing discovery as you develop and revise your work. New ideas and connections will emerge if you keep working on and thinking about your paper. See *Writing in Action: Creating an Introduction* for practice writing an introduction that will set reader's expectations for the paper.

Writing in Action: Creating an Introduction

Locate one current scholarly article on stem cell research and human cloning by using Google Scholar or one of your library's databases. Investigate who wrote the article and make sure that it was written by a medical professional or scientist. Select an article that is between 2–5 pages in length; if it is significantly longer than 5 pages, it will probably be written for an audience consisting of those in the medical profession. Read the article, and then draft an introduction to your paper with a thesis statement—the thesis should answer the questions "Are there ethical problems with human cloning? Why or why not? If there are ethical problems, to what extent should these problems impact scientific research?" Keep the guidelines in the first section of this chapter in mind to help you develop your introduction.

5.2 The Body of the Paper

The **body** is the heart of your paper, and it consists of all of the paragraphs of your essay other than your introduction and conclusion. It is where you will fulfill the promises you made in the introduction. If the introduction "tells readers what you will tell them," the body is where you "tell them." In the body of the paper, you will explain, describe, argue, explore, or elaborate on the main point or points you presented in your thesis statement, depending on the purpose of the paper. Each main idea you presented in the introduction will become a paragraph or a set of

mimagephotography/Shutterstock.com

Topic sentences should provide a clear view of the argument to be presented in a given paragraph.

paragraphs in the body of the paper, and the main ideas should be discussed in the same order you presented them in your thesis statement.

You should have somewhere between one and six main points in the body of a paper. Longer papers do not necessarily have more main points than shorter papers; they just have more detail and more explanation. Make sure to limit the amount of information you share in one paper; having too many main points can cause you and your readers to lose focus on the major idea of the paper. Students often ask, "How much of the paper should be the body, and how much space should be allotted to the introduction and the conclusion?" Again, there is not a specific formula. However, a good rule of thumb is 10/80/10. Remember that the body of your paper is where you discuss the main points you want readers to remember, so it should represent the largest part of your paper. If about 10% of your paper is devoted to the introduction, 80% of the paper to the body, and 10% to the conclusion, you will have a reasonable ratio. As a rough guide, in a three-page paper, about ⅓ of a page would be devoted to the introduction, about 2⅓ pages would be devoted to the body, and about ⅓ of a page would be devoted to the conclusion. In a much longer essay, you may write a one-page introduction and a one-page conclusion.

Again, let us use our soccer paper as an example. Our thesis statement for that paper is: "Competitive soccer has not only helped me work out my stress and stay in shape, but it has also taught me key values such as teamwork and time management that translate to other aspects of my life and work." The thesis statement promises that the paper will discuss how soccer has helped the writer deal with stress, stay in shape, learn teamwork, and improve her time management. So, the reader expects to find at least four paragraphs (or four sets of paragraphs) about each of these topics, in the order that they were mentioned in the thesis statement. These topics are the main points of the body paragraphs. See Figure 5.3 for a breakdown of the main points in our soccer paper.

Figure 5.3: Main points in body paragraphs

Crafting Topic Sentences

Each body paragraph should have a topic sentence. **Topic sentences** are mini-thesis statements, and they are typically best placed at the very beginning of each body paragraph so that the argument for that paragraph is as clear as possible. They should present your argument but in a much smaller form—you should state which single point you intend to prove in that paragraph. A strong topic sentence often mirrors some of the language in the thesis by indicating which main point you will cover. The topic sentence should reflect one point from the larger thesis statement that you can adequately prove over the course of a paragraph. Here is an example of a strong topic sentence: "One way in which Kingston relies on tradition in her novel *China Men* is by adapting tradition to American culture but retaining the tradition's original meaning." This topic sentence is offering one point on the depiction of tradition in *China Men*. For the soccer example above, the topic sentence for the first body paragraph might be, "One of the most significant ways that soccer has helped me is by giving me an outlet to work out stress."

Supplying Supporting Detail

Support the topic sentence's main point by elaborating on what you mean in the paragraph. Supporting statements can be in the form of a definition, additional detail, further explanation, or factual evidence (in the case of a more historical or political paper). Include at least one additional supporting sentence that provides detail or elaborates on your topic sentence. Examples are likely to be direct citations from the text you are writing about. However, if you are writing a personal essay, you will also include personal examples. You might only use statistics in a paper that is for a political science or sociology course, or another course in the sciences. Remember to give credit for any outside sources that you use in your papers. Several sentences of analysis should follow each quote. Analysis involves giving your "reading" or interpretation of a passage, which can include a discussion of how it seems the language is being used, what it suggests, or why it is important to the rest of the text.

Paragraph Cohesion and Transitions

In order for a paragraph to be cohesive, it should articulate a clear argument in the topic sentence, supply supporting detail and evidence, and analyze that evidence—all while actively advancing the main idea stated in the topic sentence. Only include additional quotes beyond the first one if it adds to the analysis. Look for an additional piece of evidence that is related to your main idea but that covers slightly new ground in comparison with what your first piece of evidence indicated. You can write a truly excellent body paragraph by only using a few quotes in it, and by using most of the paragraph's space for analyzing what the quotes mean. Also, in order to maintain paragraph cohesion, you should not end a paragraph with a direct quote—your job in a paper is to articulate your argument, so you must explain why you have included a quote and fully interpret it before moving on to the next paragraph. A paragraph needs closing statements from you about how the evidence you have offered supports the idea you suggested in your topic sentence.

Sometimes, one main point requires a few body paragraphs in order to sufficiently prove your point. If that is the case, divide your ideas between a main idea and a subpoint. Sometimes, the subpoint naturally emerges when the paragraph stretches beyond a page in length; reread the paragraph and ask yourself whether there is a subpoint, which is related to, but slightly different from, the main point you are discussing. If you can locate a subpoint, make that the start of a new paragraph, and work on reframing this sentence into an appropriate topic sentence for a new paragraph. It is perfectly fine if one of your main points requires two paragraphs but another main point only needs one paragraph—if you sufficiently develop and prove your points, then this structure will be appropriate.

Transitions, also called *connectives*, are words, phrases, or sentences that let readers know that you are moving from one idea to another or from one section of the paper to another. They act as a bridge to connect ideas and to indicate to readers the relationship between those ideas. You often need transitions to tie together sentences in a paragraph, to tie paragraphs to one another, and to tie sections of the paper together.

Transitions can be categorized into four different types, as shown below. As you revise, remember to insert whatever type of transition you think would be most useful to help readers follow your ideas.

1. Use signal words—transitions consisting of a single word or phrase that signal you are moving from one point to another and indicate the relationship between two ideas (Table 5.1).
   Example: When I played soccer, I made many new friends I would otherwise never have met. Additionally, I learned essential teamwork skills.

2. Mention both an idea you discussed previously and the new idea.
   Example: Now that we have discussed the ways in which soccer affected my character, let us turn our attention to how playing soccer helped shape my personal values.

3. Use advance organizers—words that indicate the structure of the material and let readers know what to expect next.
Example: We will now examine two of the most important aspects of my life that playing soccer helped to shape: my character and my values.

4. Include reminders and internal summaries to inform readers of where you are in the paper or what you have covered.
Example of a reminder: As we continue our discussion of personal values, let us turn our attention to . . . .

Example of an internal summary: We have now discussed the ways in which playing soccer helped shape my personal values.

Table 5.1: Signal words

Relationship	Signal Words
To show that an idea is in addition to the idea previously mentioned	again, also, besides, further, furthermore, in addition, too, and, next, additionally, likewise, moreover, then, in fact, finally, afterward, after that, another, indeed
To illustrate or expand a point, to give an example, or to show that an idea is similar to another idea	for instance, for example, for one thing, to illustrate, similarly, in the same way, at the same time, along the same lines, by analogy, comparably, analogous, corresponding, parallel to, coinciding with
To link cause and effect	as a result, because, therefore, thus, accordingly, consequently, in short, in summary, concurring, agreeing, just as, that is, namely, in fact, in one case, in one situation, akin to, likewise, such as, indeed, in other words, specifically, in conclusion, to conclude, for these reasons, given, then, hence, since, so
To compare two ideas in degree or quantity	more, most, fewer, less, greater than, superior, additional, further, added
To contrast two ideas or show how they are different	however, unlike, on the other had, but, yet, still, nevertheless, nonetheless, on the contrary, in contrast, by contrast, although, though, nor, albeit, instead, rather, conversely
To show time or sequence	at the same time, now, before, when, then, first, second, third, next, during, initially, finally, occasionally, frequently, meanwhile, in the meantime, soon, immediately following, eventually, as soon as, after, at that time, later, after a few hours, presently, while, not long after, at length, again, subsequently, afterward, previously, at last, in the end, currently, later, in the future, formerly, simultaneously
To indicate position or place	here, there, where, beyond, next to, nearly, close to, adjacent to, near, opposite, behind, instead

(continued)

Table 5.1: Signal words *(continued)*

Relationship	Signal Words
To show location or relationship of one idea to another	next to, behind, in front of, attached to, adjacent to, previous, prior, preceding, in relationship to
To show that one idea follows another	subsequently, ensuing, succeeding, following, next, successive, sequential, consecutive
To concede or acknowledge a point or a different opinion	though, although, nonetheless, nevertheless, still, after all, notwithstanding, even so, even though, no doubt, doubtless, certainly, of course, granted, admittedly, regardless, albeit, whereas, in spite of, at the same time, alternately, alternatively, to be sure
To qualify a statement you made (to modify it or make it less strong)	of course, perhaps, possibly, perchance, maybe, generally, usually, especially, particularly, conceivably, supposedly, if, unless, in case, provided, frequently, occasionally, in general, in particular, often
To summarize or to indicate results or conclusion	as a result, resulting, finally, therefore, then, thus, accordingly, hence, consequently, in short, in other words, in sum, ergo, in brief, in summary, to summarize, in conclusion, to conclude, for these reasons, given, wherefore, following, effect, outcome, in closing, as a finale, to end, corollary, ending, completing, terminating, finishing, repercussion, culmination, synopsis, to review, in the final analysis, in essence, on the whole, to sum up, above all, after all, all in all, in the same way, just as, at the same time, along these lines, by analogy, accordingly

Approximate Body Paragraph Balance

The information about each main point should be approximately balanced in the body of your paper. In other words, if you have one paragraph about your first main point, then you should have one paragraph or so on each of the other main points. If three or four paragraphs support the first main point, then about three or four paragraphs should also support each of the other main points.

The number of paragraphs for each point does not have to be exactly even; the goal here is balance. If a point is indeed a main point, then it should occupy approximately as much of the reader's attention as the other points. If you write one paragraph on main point 1 and five paragraphs on main point 2, readers might assume that main point 1 is of lesser importance, and your body paragraphs would not be balanced. When you are writing your paper, if you have very little to say on one of the points, consider eliminating it as a main point or combining it with another point in some way to maintain the balance in your paper.

Body Paragraph Organization

Main ideas that you present in the introduction become paragraphs or sets of paragraphs in the body of the paper, and should be discussed in the body in the same order you presented them in your thesis statement. But what is the best order to present this information? If you are writing a paper for a political science class, you may want to organize your paper according to cause and effect—what events happened first, and then later, what consequences this led to. On the other hand, if you are analyzing a novel, you likely do not want to use a chronological order. Instead, it may be more appropriate to order your points according to how a concept develops over the course of the novel. You may, for instance, begin with the definition of honesty that is offered toward the end of the novel, but then use a quote from the opening chapters of the novel to show how the definition is different at the novel's beginning. It is up to you to determine the appropriate order for developing your thoughts.

In other papers, though, the main points require a specific type of organization for the paper to be logical and flow well, and for readers to follow along with your ideas. Remember to consider the organization of main points in your paper and to choose an appropriate organizational structure. Some common structures are listed below. Whichever organizational method you select, make sure the order of main points is the same in the introduction, the thesis statement, the body of the paper, and later in the conclusion.

- *Chronological order.* With this type of organization, you present main points in the order they occurred in time, usually from earliest to latest. A chronological organization is common in narrative writing, where you are telling a story, or in other types of writing where events occur in a sequence.
- *Spatial order.* With a spatial organization, you arrange main points in a direction, from bottom to top, from up to down, from left to right, or geographically, such as from east to west or north to south. For example, if you were describing an office high-rise building, you might begin at the bottom floor and describe each floor, in order, moving up to the top of the building. If you were describing the United States, it would be more logical to organize your description spatially by discussing states in order from north to south or east to west, rather than simply mentioning them in a random order.
- *Priority order.* When you organize items or tasks in priority order, you arrange them in order of importance or the sequence in which they must be performed. Priority order is often used when you provide instructions and want to be sure steps are followed in a specific sequence. Steps are usually numbered when a priority order is used, to reinforce the fact that they must be followed consecutively.
- *Alphabetical order.* An alphabetical order may be useful for organizing lists of random items. For example, if you were preparing a list of items to pack for an emergency kit, an alphabetical order might be the most logical method of arranging the items.
- *General-to-specific order.* With complex subjects, organizing main ideas from the most general to the most specific can help readers stay on track with what you write. For instance, if you wanted to discuss different types of flowers, you might begin by discussing the growing patterns (perennials versus annuals) and then get more specific by breaking down the growing patterns into sun versus shade plants. Then you might discuss whether the plants are grown from seeds or bulbs. Finally, you might cover the specific species of flowers (primroses, pansies, dahlias, daffodils).

- *Dramatic order.* The dramatic order is described in Chapter 6, under the personal writing pattern of narration. This organizational structure is common for personal papers as well as for fictional writing.

See *Writing in Action: Creating Body Paragraphs* for practice writing well-organized body paragraphs.

Writing in Action: Creating Body Paragraphs

Return to the introduction you wrote on the ethics of human cloning. Re-read what you have written and then develop two body paragraphs in which you justify and support the argument stated in your thesis. Develop two points or main ideas and address one of these main points in each body paragraph. Include direct citation from the article you have chosen in each body paragraph and analyze the evidence for at least two sentences before you introduce another quote. After you draft your body paragraphs, re-read what you have written and evaluate your topic sentences to make sure they connect to the thesis and make an arguable claim. Keep in mind that if you state something that is simply true or false it is not an argument. Give your interpretation of the issue but connect this interpretation with a main reason or idea. Develop your paragraphs fully enough so that you are offering reasoning and examples. Define your terms carefully, such as the term "ethics." For one person, ethics may consist of what is best for the most individuals but for others ethics means doing what is best for one particular concept rather than necessarily for society as a whole.

5.3 The Conclusion

If the introduction "tells readers what you will tell them" and the body "tells them," then the conclusion "tells them why it matters." The **conclusion** brings closure to your paper so it should not restate the thesis or only summarize the main points covered in the essay. Instead, the conclusion should offer an explanation of what all of the main points *add up to*. What do these main points suggest? What larger statement can you make about the significance of this theme or concept you have explored? The conclusion does not have to be lengthy; it merely has to perform the following three functions:

Jenson/Shutterstock.com

The conclusion is where you assemble the parts of your paper into a unified whole.

1. Signal the conclusion of the paper
2. Summarize the main points of the paper
3. End on a strong note

Signal the Conclusion of the Paper

The conclusion should provide a signal to the reader that the paper is concluding. After you have discussed your main points in the body of the paper, your readers expect to have some form of closure to finish the paper. Do not leave them hanging by failing to write an effective conclusion. Remember, you can create a signal by using a transition. *Writing Samples: Sample Conclusion* illustrates a complete conclusion for our soccer paper, with all elements of the conclusion numbered and labeled in Figure 5.4.

> **Writing Samples:** Sample Conclusion
>
> Now that I have shared the various ways that playing competitive soccer has enriched my life experiences and impacted my character, I hope that you look at the value of team sports with new eyes.[1] Before you dismiss team sports as no more than a simple "hobby," consider the ways in which a sport like soccer can influence your stress levels, physical fitness, teamwork values, and time management skills.[2] Then you can choose to sign up for a fun-filled activity that will make you focused, fit, and dedicated, and maybe rack up some great wins along the way.[3]

Figure 5.4: Components of the conclusion

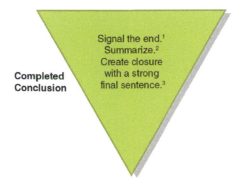

Completed Conclusion

Signal the end.[1]
Summarize.[2]
Create closure with a strong final sentence.[3]

Summarize Main Points

In some way, reinforce for your readers the main points you made in your paper. Do not simply restate your thesis statement, but rephrase the main points and reinforce them in the readers' minds. For example, if the thesis for our soccer paper is "Playing soccer helped to shape my values and character and helped make me the person I am today," the writer of the soccer paper might rephrase this thesis in the conclusion by saying, "Now that I have shared the various ways that playing competitive soccer has enriched my life experiences and impacted my character, I hope that you look at the value of team sports with new eyes."

End on a Strong Note

Make sure your paper does not just end abruptly after the last main point in the body, simply fade away, or end with a sentence such as "That is all I have to say on this subject." Use one of the strategies outlined earlier in this chapter for creating effective introductions—such as a quotation, a question, a startling statement, or an anecdote—to conclude your paper. You may also simply use strong, forceful words that craft a powerful ending for your paper. Your conclusion is your final opportunity to connect with your readers; take advantage of it.

After you address the three functions of a conclusion covered above, you can also broaden your conclusion by reflecting on the material you covered and, if appropriate, ask your readers to take action. You might also revisit the introduction and remind readers of comments you made there, restate the importance of your topic, or reflect on the implications of what you said in the paper. Generally, you should not include new citations in the conclusion because textual analysis works best in body paragraphs. The purpose of the conclusion is to create closure for the paper and to reinforce your argument. See *Writing in Action: Creating a Strong Conclusion* for practice ending your paper one a strong note.

> **Writing in Action:** Creating a Strong Conclusion
>
> Return to the essay you have been gradually developing over the course of reading this chapter. Reread your intro and body paragraphs and reflect on the points you have made so far. Develop a conclusion in which you return to your thesis and explain what the main points you discussed ultimately add up to. Make connections in respect to your two main points. Include an explanation of why this topic matters and how it is relevant to current concerns.

5.4 Structure Across Paper Types

cocozero/Shutterstock.com

Structure varies among the different types of academic papers depending on what each is meant to accomplish.

Remember that most college papers need to be approached by choosing an appropriate topic; narrowing and focusing that topic; and developing an effective introduction, body, and conclusion for the paper. Each paper type calls for a different structure, so it is important to identify the kind of paper you are being asked to write and structure it accordingly. The sections below will help you determine the appropriate structure for narrative, expository, argument, and research papers.

Structure and the Narrative Essay

For a narrative essay, you may not be asked to write argument-driven topic sentences, so the thesis statement for a narrative essay may differ from one you would write for other paper types. Rather than stating a specific claim, the thesis statement in a narrative essay may instead give a minimal amount of information in order to intrigue the reader and it may simply be descriptive in nature.

In body paragraphs, the details offered would be details that you have created for an intriguing storyline, and they might not directly connect to the topic sentence. Sometimes the best paragraphs in narrative essays create a reversal of expectations set up at the beginning of the paragraph. Likely, a mixture between this technique and a more standard form of paragraph cohesion—with ideas that develop a main idea—is the best strategy. If every single paragraph tried to surprise the reader by saying the exact opposite at the end, it would no longer be an effective strategy!

The conclusion of a narrative essay often differs from other paper types as well. While most paper types call for a summary paragraph that restates the main points of the paper, a narrative essay may instead conclude with a discussion of why the topic of interest is important. For example, the writer may discuss the reasons the topic is important to him or her, or may take a broader approach and discuss why the topic is important to society as a whole.

Structure and the Expository Essay

Expository writing shares information or explains a subject to readers. While expository essays do not usually contain an overt argument in the same way that argument and research papers do, the thesis statement should still aim to explain an issue clearly.

Although there may not be a direct thesis statement, body paragraphs should still include topic sentences, which indicate the main points of each paragraph. The body paragraphs of a well-written expository essay should also follow a logical order. Any of the previously discussed organizational structures may work for expository essays. For instance, they can be organized in the sequence in which events occur, the order in which ideas should be considered, or by the priority of the items discussed. The main points of your body paragraphs should be supported by logically ordered facts, explanations, details, or examples in order to fully explain the subject matter and maintain clarity for the reader.

Structure and the Argument Essay

This is the type of essay you will write more frequently in your college writing classes. Argumentative essays take an interpretive position and make an arguable claim in the thesis statement. These essays may offer an interpretation about a work of fiction or on a political or social issue. The interpretation is stated in the thesis and includes main points that are then developed into separate body paragraphs.

In the body paragraphs of an argument paper, assert each main point in your claim and provide evidence and reasoning to support your points. You can use examples, statistics, or the words of experts to support your statements and aid in your explanations. You may also choose to present counterarguments you think readers might make and give the reasoning behind the counterarguments as well.

The conclusion of an argument paper should reinforce or restate your thesis statement, point out a solution to the issue, or propose that your readers take some action. Provide strong closure to your argument, using the strategies for an effective conclusion discussed earlier in this chapter.

Structure and the Research Paper

Like argumentative essays, research papers articulate an interpretation that is based on some form of evidence, such as citations from a novel. Research papers use a variety of sources and include scholarly articles that extensively research a particular subject. In a research paper, therefore, the primary evidence you use will be citations from scholarly articles. Research papers must set out a clear organizational structure in the thesis statement and develop the points in clearly articulated paragraphs. Research papers also require an explanation of the historical context of the main source the writer discusses.

Chapter Summary

Every writer moves from selecting a topic to producing a polished written document in a unique way. However, good writers recognize that writing is not one task; it is a series of tasks that must be completed in a step-by-step manner. The writing process for college papers can be broken into specific steps, each of which includes specific tasks that must be performed at that particular step. Structurally, college essays consist of an introduction, enough body paragraphs to sufficiently develop an idea, and a conclusion that explains connections that can be drawn in relation to the body paragraphs. However, the nature of these individual components—the introduction, the body paragraphs, and the conclusion—varies widely depending on the specific type of essay. Thus, it is crucial to outline your essay and develop a tentative organizational plan.

For argumentative and research papers, introductions should offer context fitting for the topic and present a thesis statement that suggests the outline for the rest of the paper. The body paragraphs should in turn follow the organization laid out in the thesis statement. Narrative and expository essays frequently have introductions that are highly descriptive but they tend not to have a thesis statement. However, they still must develop an organizational method appropriate for the essay. For instance, the narrative or expository essay may go out of chronological order to present the ideas in a slightly surprising way.

Narrative, expository, argumentative, and research papers all use some form of evidence, details, or information in every body paragraph in order to develop the paper's ideas. Conclusions for these papers may synthesize the content of the previous paragraphs, discuss the larger significance of the paper topic, or, in the case of the narrative essay, may instead conclude mysteriously without all points of the storyline tied together. Regardless of the type of essay you are assigned, your papers should aim to demonstrate a progression of ideas with each new paragraph adding something new to the conversation.

Key Terms

body The section of an essay that consists of all of the paragraphs except for the introduction and conclusion. The body of the essay is the place where writers develop the thesis and prove the argument by using evidence.

conclusion The end of your discussion of the topic and the closure to your paper. The conclusion should offer an explanation of what all of the main points *add up to*.

hook The first few sentences of a paper that should capture readers' attention and interest them enough that they want to keep reading.

introduction The beginning of your discussion of the topic and the rest of the paper. A good introduction accomplishes four primary goals: captures the readers' attention and interests them in reading more; reveals the purpose of the paper and the topic; presents the thesis statement; and previews the main points covered in the body of the paper.

rhetorical question A question for which an answer is not expected because it is assumed to be obvious.

topic sentences Types of sentences that are typically placed at the beginning of each paragraph and indicate what the writer will argue or try to prove in that one paragraph.

transitions Words, phrases, or sentences that let readers know that you are moving from one idea to another or from one section of the paper to another. Also called *connectives*.

Personal Writing

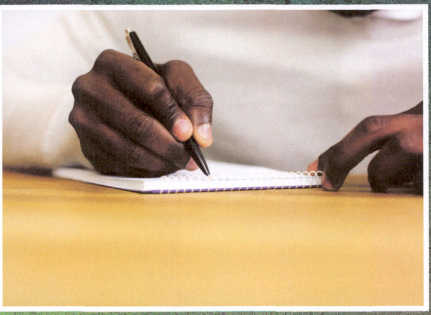

Dean Drobot/Shutterstock.com

Learning Objectives

After reading this chapter, you should be able to do the following:

1. Explain the purpose of a personal writing essay.

2. Recognize the different types of personal essays.

3. Identify the different components of a personal writing assignment, such as point of view, structure, tone, and language usage.

4. Create personal essays that are aware of the audience, have a strong plot, have a clear point, use concrete language, and properly incorporate dialogue.

5. Generate essays with great descriptions by being specific, appealing to the senses, selecting the right details, and utilizing comparisons.

Writing is a form of personal freedom. It frees us from the mass identity we see in the making all around us. In the end, writers will write not to be outlaw heroes of some underculture but mainly to save themselves, to survive as individuals.

—Don DeLillo

From *Essentials of College Writing: Contemporary Applications, 2/E* by Christine M. Connell and Kathy Sole. © 2013 Bridgepoint Education.

As you have learned, there are four primary types of college writing: personal, expository, persuasive/argument, and research assignments. You are probably familiar with personal papers because they are frequently assigned in elementary and high school. For instance, you may have written a paper describing what you did on your summer vacation, or you may have shared your impressions of a book you read or a movie you saw. In college, you will occasionally be asked to write a personal reflection or essay on a defined topic. Although personal papers may not be the most common type of writing assignment you will encounter in your college classes, you will most likely have some personal or narrative writing assignments in your courses, and many of your academic papers will be combination papers in which you must take a personal position on an issue. Perhaps you have composed an essay about a significant person or event in your life or a paper reflecting on your personal goals or what a college education means to you. Papers such as these can be defined as personal papers. Developing a personal position on a subject can help you clarify ideas, practice logical skills, and exercise your reasoning abilities.

6.1 What Is Personal Writing?

Personal writing may share a personal experience or perspective, and it can be an effective method for offering a viewpoint on a text or an event. Writing from the personal perspective may also allow a writer to write more freely than he or she otherwise would because it is less burdened by formal conventions than other types of writing. Personal writing includes opinion papers, reflective papers, response papers, creative writing assignments, and combination papers.

Red Confidential/Shutterstock.com

Personal writing allows you the freedom to express your own ideas, thoughts, and beliefs in a creative manner, often without having to adhere to the structure or conventions of other writing styles.

The Purpose of Personal Writing

Personal papers are usually written to accomplish one of the following purposes:

- Tell a story;
- Share a personal experience;
- Give a personal interpretation of an event;
- Describe a person, place, object, or event;
- Express personal feelings or opinions on a subject; or
- Entertain or provoke the audience.

When you write a personal paper, you express your own thoughts, ideas, and opinions about a subject. *Writing in Action: Week 2 Essay: Literary Elements* illustrates questions that could be asked for a personal paper on a film.

Writing in Action: Week 2 Essay: Literary Elements

Consider an interesting movie you have seen recently. Prepare a three-page paper about that movie based on the following questions:

1. Keeping in mind what you have learned in class thus far about literary elements, what does this movie mean to you?
2. What is this movie really about?
3. Is there a "moral to the story," a theme to be explored, or a comment to think about?
4. What is the point of the movie?
5. Did you find this movie meaningful for you personally? Why or why not?

Recognizing Personal Writing Assignments

Personal papers can sometimes allow you to think through your position on a topic and even aid you in writing an expository, persuasive, argumentative, or research paper. Many of the required papers in your college courses will be combination papers that are a blend of personal papers and one or more of the other types of college writing. Let us look at some assignments that fall into the category of personal papers or have personal writing components, as well as some that do not.

When It Is Not Personal

If a prompt is asking you to write an analysis, interpretation, objective account, or a research paper, it is likely not asking you to write a personal essay or to integrate personal elements. A prompt will clearly indicate that it is asking you to incorporate elements of personal writing by asking you to discuss your feelings, experiences, memories, impressions, or perspective. Ask yourself whether the assignment in any way is about you as a person—if it is, then you should include personal elements, and if it is not, then no personal elements should be used. Table 6.1 provides a list of words in an essay prompt that would signal that the essay is not personal (but make sure it is not a combination essay and doesn't ask you to relate something from your personal life. See the examples given in the sections "Opinion Papers" and "Combination Papers").

Table 6.1: Key words in an essay prompt that signal nonpersonal writing

Give an *objective* account . . .
Assess the *factual* circumstances . . .
Offer an *interpretation* . . .
Produce a *reading*. . .
Research the historical underpinnings of . . .
Evaluate the consequences of the newly passed legislation . . .
Argue for the significance of the text's theme of justice . . .

Keep in mind that Table 6.1 is not a complete list; look for terms in the writing prompt that gesture toward objectivity or reasoned interpretation. If you are unsure whether or not a prompt allows for any personal elements whatsoever, ask your instructor, but bear in mind that the prompt will explicitly ask for this if it is what is required of you. The following *Writing in Action* box, *Personal Paper Assignments*, provides examples of paper prompts that specifically ask the writer to compose a personal paper.

Writing in Action: Personal Paper Assignments

You can recognize a personal paper assignment by key words or phrases in the assignment that ask you for your opinion or your views on a subject. Key words and action verbs are underlined in the following examples:

- Write about an experience in which you struggled with something and were unsuccessful and discuss what you learned from the experience.
- Explain what you think about a current scientific or social controversy.
- Reflect on a person who had a strong impact on your life and the ways in which he or she influenced you.
- Imagine that you have unlimited wealth and write about what you would do with your money and why.
- What do you think has been the most important social or political movement of the 20th century?

Opinion Papers

Opinion papers express the writer's point of view or opinion on a specific topic. They may be personal papers if you are asked simply to give your opinion on an issue and explain your point of view. An **opinion** is a personal viewpoint on a subject that may or may not be supported with facts or evidence. However, if you are required to state your opinion and then argue that point of view, your paper will be a combination of personal and persuasive writing. This would be a hybrid paper that asks you to incorporate both personal reflection and logical, nonpersonal argumentation. If you are writing this kind of paper, you should keep the personal and argumentative sections of the paper separate in order to show how your personal reflections contributed to your argument. This will also help ensure that you include an argumentative, nonpersonal section to your paper. For example, an opinion assignment may ask you to write an essay in which you discuss whether or not you think you should buy products from a company who gives money to something you do not personally support.

Reflective Papers

Personal papers may also be assigned when your instructors want you to think about something you have read and to respond to it or discuss its meaning for you; these assignments are often called **reflective papers**. However, if an assignment asks you to reflect, discuss, or explain something, be careful. The words *reflect*, *discuss*, and *explain* all have multiple meanings.

We reflect on something when we think about it and express our personal opinion or share a personal story. However, the word *reflect* can also mean to carefully consider something or to explore options. Instead of voicing your own opinion, a reflective paper assignment may be asking you to consider an issue, to analyze a situation, or to explore options, based on what you have learned in the course. This type of assignment requires an expository paper, which we will discuss in Chapter 7. Similarly, if an assignment asks you to discuss or explain an issue, you must look further at the assignment to determine whether you are being asked to write a personal paper that discusses or explains your own opinion or whether you are being asked to share information you have learned from your text or from research. A reflective paper, for instance, may ask you to read an article on a current event and then to reflect on the position stated there.

Response Papers

When you are asked to respond to material you have read by expressing your personal opinion on a topic or to reflect on what you have read and share its meaning for you, your instructors are looking for a specific type of response from you. Responses to reading, like other personal papers, require that you state your opinion on an issue or reflect on an issue and state your viewpoint about it, and they are written in first person. However, unlike other personal papers, you do not choose the subject. Before you write a response, you have most likely read about or discussed a controversial topic. A **response paper** usually requires you to think about the different points of view expressed in the material you read or discussed and to take a personal stand on the issue. Because a response paper asks you to begin by demonstrating that you understand the issue, it is usually best to begin with the more objective third person. Notice that this is very different from the suggested format discussed earlier for the combination personal and research paper.

In this type of paper, you generally begin by presenting a brief overview of the issue and the different viewpoints presented, to demonstrate that you understand both the issue itself and the controversy surrounding it. This first part of the paper is expository (see Chapter 7) and should therefore be written in third person. Then, you will switch to a first-person point of view and share your opinion of the issue and state where you stand on the issue. This part of the paper requires personal writing. Finally, you must support your point of view by stating why you believe as you do and how you came to adopt this perspective. Discuss what factors were most important to you in arriving at a conclusion about the issue.

As you can see, papers that ask you to respond to reading share all the characteristics of other personal papers outlined earlier in this chapter, but they also require that you explore and explain your opinion, which is often a way to introduce you to expository writing. A response paper could ask you to read two positions on the creation of constitutional amendments—one for and one against— and then to develop a personal response that indicates your viewpoint.

Creative Writing Assignments

The term **creative writing** refers to written works or artistic expressions whose purpose is to create images or to express thoughts or feelings. It can also include information and an implied or direct position. Creative writing can be considered personal writing and includes genres, or categories, of writing such as short stories, novels, poetry, screenplays, and creative **nonfiction** like biographies and memoirs. You may engage in creative writing as part of your college career if you take a dedicated creative writing course, if one of your other courses has an assignment that involves creative writing, or if you decide to pursue creative writing as an extracurricular activity. Journaling, and idea-generating techniques like mind mapping and free-writing, covered in Chapter 4, are also examples of personal creative writing.

Combination Papers

A **combination paper** may require you to combine elements of personal, expository, persuasive or argument, and research papers. For example, you may have an assignment that asks you to state your opinion on a controversial issue (personal) and then to conduct research and find evidence both in support of and in opposition to your viewpoint (research). This type of assignment combines elements of personal and research writing in the same paper. In a combination paper such as this, you will write in first person when you are stating your personal opinion and then switch to third person when you report the information you found in your research. This would be an appropriate format if the assignment asks you to first convey your personal opinion and then to lay out and develop your reasoning afterward. The first person "I" is not appropriate when you discuss research because research is not personal but rather an objective interpretation. This means that while others may have a different interpretation of the same research, it is not "personal" to state your interpretation—therefore, the first person "I" is inappropriate. A combination paper could ask you to do research about the extent to which American citizens should have the freedom of speech before it begins to infringe on the rights of others and then to formulate a viewpoint on this subject using the first person.

6.2 Personal Writing Conventions

Before responding to a personal writing assignment, it is important to understand how to construct a personal paper. Personal writing generally calls for writing conventions that differ from those used in other types of writing, such as argument and exposition. For example, the tone, language, and structure used in a personal paper are often more informal than in other paper types. The following sections will help guide you in choosing the proper tone, language, point of view, and structure for writing a personal paper.

Tone and Language

Personal papers are generally written in a less formal, or even conversational, tone, and the use of contractions and other types of informal language is often allowed, if it is appropriate to the story or the topic. Personal papers might also include dialogue, which should be placed in quotation marks. However, it is important to remember that you are writing for an academic audience and that the essay prompt may require you to include an introduction and a thesis statement that makes a claim about the personal experience you describe. The language in personal writing assignments should be appropriate, and the paper must meet the writing requirements outlined in your course guide or syllabus. If you are unsure of the type of language that is appropriate for a particular writing assignment, make sure that you ask your instructor.

RetroClipArt/Shutterstock.com

The chosen style of narration can have a significant effect on the tone and effectiveness of personal writing. Mark Twain's *Huckleberry Finn* is defined by the potentially unreliable narration of its young and uneducated title character.

Point of View

Because you are sharing your personal viewpoint on a subject, a personal paper is usually written from a first-person point of view, which means you are able to use pronouns such as *I*, *me*, *my*, *we*, and *our*. However, personal papers are often narrative and tell a story. In your paper, you might also tell a story about another person. In this instance, as the narrator, you would write from a third-person point of view and refer to the person by name or use the pronouns *he*, *she*, or *they*. This creates the effect of a more distant narrator, one who seems to be more objective precisely because the paper does not use the first person "I" and therefore does not seem to be speaking from personal opinion. Your instructor will not likely ask you to write a creative writing piece such as a short story, but the following fiction excerpt from Mark Twain's *The Adventures of Huckleberry Finn* (1895) includes several of the key elements of a personal paper. Read *Writing in Action: Excerpt From The Adventures of Huckleberry Finn* for an example of how Twain employs a first-person point of view to create a narrative from the perspective of a young boy growing up in the antebellum South. In the excerpt, Huck is trying to decide if he should do what he believes to be his duty and mail a letter reporting the whereabouts of Jim, who has escaped from slavery.

Writing in Action: Excerpt From *The Adventures of Huckleberry Finn*

I felt good and all washed clean of sin for the first time I had ever felt so in my life, and I knowed I could pray now. But I didn't do it straight off, but laid the paper down and set there thinking—thinking how good it was all this happened so, and how near I come to being lost and going to hell. And went on thinking. And got to thinking over our trip down the river; and I see Jim before me all the time: in the day and in the night-time, sometimes moonlight, sometimes storms, and we a-floating along, talking and singing and laughing. But somehow I couldn't seem to strike no places to harden me against him, but only the other kind. I'd see him standing my watch on top of his'n, 'stead of calling me, so I could go on sleeping; and see him how glad he was when I come back out of the fog; and when I come to him again in the swamp, up there where the feud was; and such-like times; and would always call me honey, and pet me and do everything he could think of for me, and how good he always was; and at last I struck the time I saved him by telling the men we had small-pox aboard, and he was so grateful, and said I was the best friend old Jim ever had in the world, and the *only* one he's got now; and then I happened to look around and see that paper.

It was a close place. I took it up, and held it in my hand. I was a-trembling, because I'd got to decide, forever, betwixt two things, and I knowed it. I studied a minute, sort of holding my breath, and then says to myself:

"All right, then, I'll *go* to hell"—and tore it up.

Structure and Supporting Ideas

Personal papers are read sequentially from beginning to end, and frequently narrate events or circumstances in chronological order, as they would occur logically in time. Personal papers do not usually contain headings to divide one section of the paper from another (if you were writing a novel or short story, however, it would be appropriate to divide up your thoughts according to organized chapters or sections). Your intent should be to capture the reader's attention at the very beginning of the paper and to carry the reader along with you, in a clear and organized way, through the end of the paper. All good personal papers share some common features. They have a suitable topic articulated over the course of several paragraphs, and they anticipate a reader's desire for context, information, and development. Consider what would be interesting to you as a reader and what kinds of details and information you look for when you read a piece of personal writing. What allows you as a reader to stay engaged with personal writing?

6.3 Narrative Writing Pattern

Narration is storytelling from the perspective of a narrator, and the story may be true, false, imaginary, or a combination. A narration can be about past, present, or future events, and it can be short or the length of a novel—it is important to note that more complex narrative forms of writing frequently combine a variety of time frames. For the purposes of your own writing, which will usually consist of a short assignment of approximately two to five pages, it is ideal to narrate from the perspective of one time frame. The event, or **plot**, of the narration may come from your own personal experience, or it may be a hypothetical situation or an event that you imagine. If the assignment states that you can make up a hypothetical or imaginary situation, then that is assumed and is fair to do so in your writing. However, if the assignment calls for a narrative based on something that actually occurred, be sure to select an actual event and stick to the facts of that event in writing your paper.

The Purpose of Narrative

The purpose of a narrative may be simply to entertain or engage the reader, or the story might have a more specific purpose such as to share a personally significant event or to teach a lesson, or moral. When we tell a story using a narration strategy, we attempt to bring the subject and the events to life for readers so that they can share in the experience and the emotions of the experience. To accomplish this goal, we must make sure to incorporate certain important elements in the narrative. Most of us remember being told stories as children, and we love a good story that holds our interest. We have also probably known someone who is a poor storyteller, who rambles on or gives too much detail, who goes off track, or who ruins the ending. For our narration to have impact, we must tell a story that grabs and holds the audience's attention, provides important and appropriate details, and discusses events in a clear and well-organized sequence.

Consider the Audience

When you write narrative papers, remember to think about the writing situation and consider the purpose and the audience for your paper. You might be interested in the topic, but is it appropriate for the assignment you have been given and for an academic audience? Also consider aspects of the rhetorical context such as the backgrounds and the attitudes of the audience. Anticipate how the audience is likely to react to your narrative. Will they like or dislike what you write? How do you want them to feel when they have read the story? Answers to these questions can help you determine what to write and how to write it.

Develop the Thesis

Review Chapter 5 for information on how to construct an effective thesis. Recall that a thesis statement is a claim that the writer must argue and prove over the course of an essay. All good narrations make a point and have a clear purpose. Do not leave readers wondering, "So what?" after they have read your paper. Make sure that they understand the significance of your story and the primary idea you want to share with them. In other words, why is the story important? If the assignment is asking you to articulate your personal position, then you should write a thesis that will suggest why your position is important. In this case, you would also write topic sentences that link up with the thesis statement and claims that interpret evidence. However, if you are writing fiction or a short narrative, it usually will not contain a direct thesis statement, and will likely convey significance in the story through the articulation of a key theme or concept that the story builds toward and resolves to some extent. If your story has a message such as a lesson or a moral, also make sure that the message is clear to the reader either through an explicit argument (in the form of a thesis and well-argued paragraphs) or an implicit argument (through the careful structuring of a theme or issue).

Develop the Plot

As you learned earlier, *plot* is the order, or sequence, of events that unfold in your story. It is crucial that you organize these events so that, by the end of the story, they make sense to the reader and build up to a crucial moment in the narrative. Your story should have some creative tension, and decisions about how to organize events often depend on how you want to incorporate that creative tension into the story.

Creative tension is the stress and interest created when a story has an unresolved problem or disagreement, a decision that must be made, or a dilemma or conflict that must be resolved. Without creative tension, a story is boring. Stories that incorporate creative tension capture and hold our interest. You build tension when your story includes surprising events, when an action leads to an unexpected consequence, or when factors complicate an issue and must be sorted out before they can be resolved. Include creative tension such as this in your narrative and carefully consider when to reveal key information and when to hold it back. Also make certain to resolve that creative tension by the end of your story. It is a careful balancing act: too much creative tension could result in undercommunication with the audience, but revealing everything will likely make the story a bit dull.

Anticipate and Answer Possible Reader Questions

When telling a story, do not leave your readers hanging by failing to answer important questions they may have while they read. As you create your narrative, anticipate what readers will need to know and include this information in the story. Remember what your needs are as a reader of a narrative and try to take that into consideration as you write. For instance, it is likely that you appreciate the appropriate context, background, and enough content to understand what is happening in the narrative, so you should assume your readers will as well.

Use Language and Dialogue Effectively

Effective personal writing includes using specific, concrete language that allows the audience to imagine with their senses. A writer's use of dialogue can enrich a personal narrative or creative story.

Concrete Language

Words can be categorized as either abstract or concrete. **Abstract words** such as *freedom*, *peace*, *love*, and *success* have no physical substance; we cannot see, hear, touch, smell, or taste them. **Concrete words**, on the other hand, represent people, places, and things we can see, hear, touch, smell, or taste. Concrete words such as *book*, *child*, *apple*, and *ice* are specific and tangible, and they represent physical objects rather than ideas, qualities, or concepts. They conjure up pictures in our minds of our own experiences with these objects. Good narration often utilizes the writing pattern of description, discussed later in this chapter, to ensure that readers have a clear mental picture of the story's setting or scene and its characters. Try to paint pictures by using concrete words that describe physical objects and people and help readers visualize or imagine what you want them to see.

Effective Dialogue

In narration, **dialogue** is a verbal exchange between two or more characters in a text. You can make characters come to life and give them personalities by incorporating dialogue in your narration and letting them tell the story in their own words. Writing dialogue effectively takes practice. It is useful to look at examples of dialogue in texts to see how it operates. Notice the dialogue in James McBride's autobiographical narrative "Shul/School":

> One afternoon I came home from school and cornered Mommy while she was cooking dinner. "Ma, what's a tragic mulatto?" I asked.
>
> Anger flashed across her face like lightning and her nose, which tends to redden and swell in anger, blew up like a balloon. 'Where'd you hear that?' she asked.
>
> "I read it in a book."
>
> "For God's sake, you're no tragic mul—What book is this?"
>
> "Just a book I read."
>
> "Don't read that book anymore." She sucked her teeth. "Tragic mulatto. What a stupid thing to call somebody! Somebody called you that?"
>
> "No."
>
> "Don't ever use that term."
>
> "Am I black or white?"
>
> "You're a human being," she snapped. "Educate yourself or you'll be a nobody!" (McBride, 1996/2008, p. 482)

In this excerpt from "Schul/School," dialogue serves to directly confront the issue of race as it is experienced by McBride. This dialogue conveys to the reader what the experience may have felt like from the viewpoint of McBride as a child, not McBride the adult who is reflecting back on the experience. If McBride had written this from the perspective of an adult narrating this experience in paragraph form, it simply would not be as powerful. Here, the dialogue form allows us as readers to feel as if we are part of the moment, wondering how someone could be called a "mulatto," and how that differs from McBride's own sense of himself.

Maintain Clear Narrative Order

Writers use a number of different strategies to organize information and, often, the choice of how to organize is based on your judgment of what would be most effective. Below are some organizational strategies to consider as you plan your paper and present the material. You are not required to use one of these arrangements; just be sure that your paper flows well and is organized logically. As described in Chapter 5, two of the possible ways of organizing a narrative are *chronological order* and *spatial order*. Events arranged in a chronological order are organized by time, and may start with the earliest event and go forward in time to the present or start from the present and go backward in time. Information arranged according to spatial order is organized by direction—for example, left to right, north to south, or up to down. A third organizational structure that has great significance for narrative is dramatic order or structure.

The *dramatic structure* is common in many short stories, novels, screenplays, and other types of creative writing. It can also be used effectively in your personal papers. The dramatic structure has five elements, which are described below:

1. the *opening paragraphs*, which establish the setting and characters and introduce the situation that contains the creative tension;
2. the *rising action*, which takes up the majority of the story and includes the interaction and/or dialogue between the characters, the building of tension, and the introduction of other elements of the story;
3. the *climax* or *turning point*, the moment in which the conflict comes into sharp focus and is resolved;
4. the *falling action*, or aftermath, where the rest of the story falls into place; and
5. the *concluding paragraphs or sections*, where some of the loose ends are wrapped up and the story is brought to a close. Note that you do not need to resolve everything, and in fact trying to do so might sound reductive. You should, however, provide some resolution to the main concern of the narrative.

See *Writing Sample: Soccer Personal Essay* for an example of the personal soccer paper we began in Chapters 4 and 5. Notice how each paragraph focuses on one main idea that supports the thesis, while the author also maintains a clear narrative order using the chronological arrangement to lead the reader from her early experiences playing soccer to how soccer has made her the person she is today.

Writing Sample: *Soccer Personal Essay*

What is the most fulfilling part about playing competitive soccer? Perhaps you guessed winning trophies, adrenaline highs, or staying in great shape. But in my experience, bonding with teammates and learning how to be a true team player tops the list. Thinking back on my many years as a soccer player, I have realized how important the game of soccer has been in developing my greatest friendships, along with a positive attitude towards teamwork that has in turn influenced other aspects of my life. Playing soccer has caused me to grow as a person, influencing my values and the outlook on life I have today.

For one thing, soccer has helped me to make friendships that have lasted throughout the stages of my life. I remember loving soccer from day one, even if I barely understood the concept of the game. When I was just 6 years old, my mother signed me up for a local AYSO team (American Youth Soccer Organization) that played around the corner from our church. I had always been a spunky and energetic little girl, preferring to climb trees rather than play with Barbie dolls, but soccer brought out something new in me. Suddenly, I had to learn the rules of the game, and to learn how to work with a bunch of other girls that I just met. In that first year or two, it was all about being together with my teammates, kicking around the small black-and-white ball, wondering what we would eat for snack time, and pulling up grass with our fingers. Luckily, a couple of those girls grew into two of my best friends. Now that we are starting our own families, we can think back on those days and get excited about signing up our own children for soccer one day.

Continuing to play soccer throughout my life has also taught me a great deal about what it means to work hard *and* work as a team. Unlike some of the girls from AYSO, I kept playing soccer in middle school and high school and beyond, and it was during these years that soccer began to challenge me and shape me. Many people don't realize the incredible commitment that is required when you play a competitive team sport. First, there's the fact that you practice almost every day, which is physically draining. When I would return home from a long day of school and soccer practice, that's when my homework and chores would only just begin. But in order to be at your peak condition and help your team when they need you on the field, you have to find the time and energy to handle it all. Spending so much time with the girls on my team taught us how to function as a unit. We knew we could count on each other, whether it was to show up for practice on time, help defend our goal during a game, or grab an ice pack for a teammate's injury. Being a team player isn't something that I left behind on the high school soccer field. When our son Toby was born 3 years ago, my husband Jayden and I had to support one another more than ever before, juggling our family, jobs, and finances. Like soccer, becoming a parent has been the ultimate challenge and yet so rewarding at the same time.

Soccer has also allowed me to have a familiar path toward fitness and wellness that I can take any time that I begin to feel out of shape or unhealthy. Now that I'm in my thirties and am raising my first child, it hasn't always been easy to find time to exercise, or to make my health a priority. But while I'm shorter on time than ever these days, soccer taught me to value my dedication to physical activity and health. So a year after Toby was born, I joined a local adult team, partly to try to lose some of the baby weight and get back into shape. Now, my old jeans are finally starting to fit again, and I made friends with another new mom whose son is the same age as mine. When I could easily have been overwhelmed by new responsibilities and put my health on the back burner, my soccer background helped me stay disciplined and focused.

(continued)

Writing Sample: *Soccer Personal Essay (continued)*

Overall, I would not be the person I am today without the years I spent playing competitive soccer. Not only did I learn to love the game itself, but I also learned how to make friends, be part of team, balance my time, and stay positive and healthy in multiple aspects of my life. While I'm sure I could have learned these lessons without playing soccer, I would not have learned them to the same degree. Those many days of sweat, late nights, singing on the bus, and games won and lost have stayed with me over the years. I still love soccer to this day, and cannot wait for the time to come when I can buy Toby his first jersey and pair of cleats.

6.4 Descriptive Writing Pattern

Description is a pattern of writing that can be defined as painting pictures with words. When we describe a person, place, object, or event, we provide details about its physical characteristics. As we discussed earlier, description and narration are often used together because description helps make the story we are narrating clearer and more vivid.

Nejron Photo/Shutterstock.com

Descriptive writing avoids general words in favor of the specific. It is far more effective to describe your individual instruments than to refer generally to your musical equipment.

The Purpose of Description

Effective description requires using carefully chosen language that creates the visual image you want readers to have of your story's subject. However, you can use description in other types of writing besides narration. For example, in a persuasive paper, you might use description to help readers understand the seriousness of a problem before you attempt to convince them to take action to solve that problem.

Use Specific Language

To be descriptive, use specific terms and avoid vague and general words. Break the poor writing habit of using vague, informal "catch all" words such as *things*, *stuff*, and *lots of*. Instead of writing "I have lots of music stuff and other things in my room," be specific and name each object or write a general statement and then expand it by specifically naming the various objects. For instance, you might write, "I have several musical instruments in my room including a guitar, a saxophone, and a set of drums, along with my radio and portable media player." In all forms of writing, avoid using passive voice, forms of the verb "be." For instance, if someone says, "Snacks are being eaten," the word "being" is a form of the word "be" and is passive. Passive voice often adds unnecessary words and creates ambiguity at the sentence level: Instead, use a descriptive verb to indicate precisely what you mean. To take out passive voice, you could say, "Jennifer is eating snacks," which directly identifies the subject of the sentence as actively doing something.

Select Specific Details

Good description includes important details that help paint the picture for the reader by "filling in the blanks" in the visual image. Details help you focus the reader's attention on characteristics that make people, places, objects, and events unique and help them "come alive" for readers. Look beyond the obvious for specific characteristics of what you are describing to help readers "see" it too.

Let us imagine, for example, that you are asked to describe your office workspace. You would probably begin with a description of the size and shape of your desk and the objects around the desk. But then you should look beyond the obvious and try to find specific characteristics of your workspace that make it unique from that of other workspaces. Try to elaborate on the basic description with carefully selected details that give readers a sense of the person who occupies that space.

For example, you might write, "The basic black-and-white décor of the cubicle is shattered by bold splashes of fire engine red, forest green, and pale yellow. Bright red coffee cups are strategically placed within easy reach of the computer and hold pens, paper clips, rubber bands, and other assorted necessities. The mugs contrast sharply with the four dark green sets of file folders neatly arranged, alphabetically by topic, in stacking black metal file holders. However, dozens of tiny yellow Post-it" notes disrupt the sense of organization as they litter the computer screen and desk with reminders about everything from meetings and project deadlines to groceries and family birthdays." It is precisely these specific details and uses of descriptive language that make these words more than just words—they become an imagistic scene the reader can visualize.

Use Descriptive Language

When you use description in personal writing, you seek to involve readers in the story by helping them see, hear, touch, smell, or taste what you are telling them. You do this by using language that elicits emotional responses from your readers. Words can have different connotations, or emotional impact. In most of your college writing, you want to choose words that discuss or explain issues without stirring emotions. However, in personal writing, the opposite is true; you want to deliberately choose words that paint a picture, evoke sensory experience, or that stir the reader's emotions.

For example, if you want to paint a negative picture of an alley in a rundown part of town, rather than simply stating that it "smells bad because it is littered with junk and rotting garbage," you might take readers on a journey with you down this alley by describing it this way: "As I tripped over bent and rusted tin cans, jagged pieces of broken glass, and large plastic bags of unknown contents, the putrid smell of rotting food filled my nose. Suddenly, I found myself swatting huge, black horseflies that swarmed around me." Can you visualize that alley better now?

Descriptive language refers to words that are vivid, expressive, and highly specific to the topic you are writing on. Instead of stating that you smelled a strong odor, you might specifically describe it by saying that it was *pungent*, *bitter*, *sweet*, or *spicy*. Paint a clear picture of sensations and emotions for the reader as well. For instance, rather than writing that you were angry, you might use the words *livid*, *enraged*, or *fuming with anger* to discuss your feelings—or better yet, you could explain a facial expression that conveys anger rather than simply saying you were "enraged." Table 6.2 provides you with some descriptive alternatives to common verbs, adjectives, and adverbs. Use the alternative words in this list to help make your writing more vivid. Descriptive language tends to express an evaluation of something. Because it expresses an evaluation or perspective, there is no such thing as completely objective description. However, the best description would be one that is carefully informed and that does not exaggerate ("He is absolutely always happy") or understate ("Though he is an Honors student, he is really only average in his performance"). Description should aim for accuracy and fairness and avoid exaggeration for the purpose of effect.

Table 6.2: Alternatives to common verbs, adjectives, and adverbs

Instead of *see*, write	Instead of *say* or *tell*, write	Instead of *ask*, write
spy	cry	beg
spot	yell	query
observe	shout	plead
notice	exclaim	appeal
perceive	whisper	inquire
witness	scream	request
glance	bellow	question
detect	bark	demand
discern	holler	implore
glimpse	roar	
recognize	shriek	
Instead of *eat*, write	**Instead of *run* or *go*, write**	**Instead of *like*, write**
munch	fly	adore
swallow	job	admire
consume	flee	respect
devour	race	worship
gobble	dart	appreciate
gorge	dash	value
wolf	rush	treasure
chomp	bound	cherish
chew	scurry	regard
gnaw	scamper	idolize
nibble	sprint	treasure
	hurry	relish

(continued)

Table 6.2: Alternatives to common verbs, adjectives, and adverbs *(continued)*

Instead of *look*, write	Instead of *take*, write	Instead of *think*, write
gaze	grasp	believe
stare	capture	reflect
glance	seize	imagine
glare	catch	consider
glimpse	pocket	contemplate
peep	grab	ponder
peek	pilfer	deliberate
gape	snatch	meditate
gawk	lift	mull over
scrutinize	pinch	ruminate
survey	steal	muse
study	nab	wonder

Instead of *angry*, write	Instead of *pretty*, write	Instead of *happy*, write
livid	cute	giddy
enraged	adorable	elated
fuming	attractive	pleased
irritated	beautiful	glad
irate	alluring	joyful
heated	glamorous	cheerful
annoyed	handsome	blissful
furious	lovely	ecstatic
incensed	charming	delighted
outraged	endearing	jovial
infuriated	appealing	amused
	gorgeous	excited

Instead of *good* or *great*, write	Instead of *bad*, write	Instead of *sad*, write
huge	evil	glum
immense	awful	depressed
enormous	terrible	gloomy
grand	dreadful	miserable
outstanding	appalling	heartbreaking
commendable	shocking	distressing
magnificent	ghastly	sorrowful
impressive	horrific or horrible	poignant
remarkable	deceitful	moving
notable	dire	disheartening
imposing	wicked	discouraging
inspiring	poor	gloomy
splendid	inferior	disappointing

(continued)

Table 6.2: Alternatives to common verbs, adjectives, and adverbs *(continued)*

Instead of *smart*, write	Instead of *nice*, write	Instead of *big*, write
wise	pleasant	huge
gifted	kind	large
clever	polite	enormous
intelligent	agreeable	gigantic
bright	pleasing	giant
brainy	lovely	immense
sharp	amiable	vast
quick	friendly	sizeable
informed	likable	massive
astute	affable	colossal
perceptive	gracious	tremendous
incisive	sociable	towering
insightful	cordial	soaring

Compare the Unfamiliar to the Familiar

One useful way to help readers visualize what you are describing is to compare it to something they might already know. For example, suppose you are describing a flower. You could comment on the color and the size of the flower by saying that it is pink and tiny. However, the color pink has many different shades, and the word *tiny* has a wide range of interpretations. So, instead you might state, "The color of the flower was the same hue as that of the pink candy Valentine's Day hearts."

When you report your observations of something; share personal experiences; or describe a person, place, object, or event, remember to use the elements of effective description to make your ideas clear and vivid to your readers. Read the combination narration and description essay by professional writer Anna Quindlen (2007) found at http://www .newsweek.com/id/32467/page/1. This essay illustrates many of the characteristics of effective narration and description we have discussed in this chapter. See if you can identify the strategies she uses to paint a picture of her beloved dog. On a separate sheet of paper, generate a list of strategies you see operating in the essay.

Chapter Summary

At times your discussion-post assignments may be personal writing assignments, and other writing assignments will be combination papers that have one or more sections that must be written using personal writing patterns, so it is necessary to know how this form of writing differs from expository, persuasive, and argument papers.

Personal papers ask you to express your own thoughts, ideas, and opinions about a subject. They can be written to tell a story about yourself or others; to describe a person, place, object, or event; or to express personal opinions on an issue. They may be called essays, opinion papers, reflective papers, or creative writing assignments. Personal papers, or the personal sections of a combination paper, have three important characteristics:

1. They are generally written from a first-person point of view, unless you are narrating a story about another person.
2. They are logically organized and do not have headings that interrupt the flow of the writing.
3. They are written in a conversational tone that is appropriate for an academic audience and may contain dialogue.

Personal writing often uses specific writing patterns. Each of these patterns—including narration, description, and responses to reading—has its own specific elements, which you must incorporate if your personal writing is to be effective. While narrative essays should communicate a clear purpose such as in the case of articulating a position, creative writing pieces may not contain either a direct or an implied thesis. Descriptive writing is the use of vivid, imagistic language that incorporates the senses, so in order to write descriptively, one should use language that pertains to all of the senses. This also allows readers to visualize the scene the writer creates. Because personal writing uses your imagination or asks you to reflect on your own experiences and viewpoints, it can be a useful tool to help stimulate your creativity and to give you valuable experience in expressing your ideas in written form.

Key Terms

abstract words Words that have no physical substance; we cannot see, hear, touch, smell, or taste them.

concrete words Words that represent people, places, and things we can see, hear, touch, smell, or taste; they are specific and tangible, and represent physical objects rather than ideas, qualities, or concepts.

combination paper An assignment that includes elements of personal, expository, persuasive or argument, and research papers. For instance, one section of the paper might be personal, while another is persuasive.

creative tension The stress and interest created when a story has an unresolved problem or disagreement, a decision that must be made, or a dilemma or conflict that must be resolved.

creative writing Written or artistic works whose purpose is to create images or to express thoughts or feelings. These works may also imply a position or argument.

description A pattern of writing that involves providing details about the physical character-istics of a person, place, object, or event.

descriptive language Words that are vivid, expressive, and highly specific to the topic you are writing on.

dialogue A verbal exchange between two or more characters in a text.

narration Storytelling from the perspective of a narrator. The story may be true, false, imagi-nary, or a combination.

nonfiction A genre of writing that includes biographies, memoirs, and historical documents.

opinion A personal viewpoint on a subject that may or may not be supported with facts or evidence.

opinion paper A type of essay that explains the writer's point of view or opinion on a spe-cific topic.

plot The order, or sequence, of events that unfold in a story.

reflective paper An assignment that asks the writer think about something he or she has read and to respond to it or discuss its meaning for him or her.

response paper An assignment that requires the writer to think about the different points of view expressed in the material being discussed and to take a personal stand on the issue.

Exposition

fizkes/Shutterstock.com

Learning Objectives

After reading this chapter, you should be able to do the following:

1. Explain the common purposes behind an expository essay.

2. Describe the proper and improper use of elements such as point of view, structure, and tone.

3. Differentiate between the definition, classification, and description of expository essays.

4. Recognize and know when to use informative writing.

5. Recognize and know when to use reflective writing.

6. Plan an expository essay by understanding the patterns involved in comparison-and-contrast writing.

7. Plan an expository essay by understanding the patterns involved in cause-and-effect writing.

8. Plan an expository essay by understanding the patterns involved in analytical writing.

When I'm explaining something to you, if I'm being long-winded, and twisty in a non-productive way, I could make you feel vaguely insulted. And you'd have a right to be.

—George Saunders

From *Essentials of College Writing: Contemporary Applications, 2/E* by Christine M. Connell and Kathy Sole. © 2013 Bridgepoint Education.

When you browse newspapers or magazines, surf the Web for information, read business reports and memos, look through a cookbook or catalog, or follow instructions to assemble a child's toy, you are viewing examples of exposition. Exposition conveys information or explains a subject to readers. It is often assigned in college to expose you to new subjects and to allow you to demonstrate your understanding of these subjects. You will find exposition and expository writing not only in college classes but also at the workplace and in your personal life.

Technical writing and business and professional writing are also specialized categories of expository writing that involve communicating complex information to users for specific purposes. You will not be expected to produce many of these types of materials in college unless you take specific courses in these subjects. However, whenever you are asked to prepare instructions, step-by-step directions to perform an operation, or procedures for accomplishing a task, remember to apply the elements of exposition. The pages that follow will discuss key features of expository writing, including their conventions, and will offer detailed information about specific forms of expository writing most typical to the college classroom—informative writing, reflective writing, comparison-and-contrast essays, cause-and-effect essays, and analytical papers.

7.1 Understanding Expository Writing

Exposition, or expository writing, is writing with the purpose of describing, explaining, or analyzing. It is one of the most common types of writing you will encounter in your college courses. Many of your college assignments will require you to read exposition, to write expository papers, or to use exposition for sections of a paper. In fact, this text is an example of exposition. The primary purpose of exposition is to share information. Exposition is used for a variety of specific reasons, some of which are listed below:

- Inform readers about a topic
- Clarify or explain a theory, concept, or idea
- Define terms and their uses
- Analyze an issue
- Instruct readers in how to perform a task
- Objectively describe an item
- Explore or evaluate ideas
- Summarize ideas
- Interpret a subject so that readers understand it.

Because most issues must be discussed or explained before they can be argued or researched, exposition will also be a component of many combination papers you will write in your college courses. Before you share a personal experience (personal paper), take a position on an issue (persuasive paper), or conduct research to learn more about a subject (research paper), you must usually explain the subject, define relevant terms, and provide background information about your topic. The elements of exposition are important to success in all your college courses.

Recall that we have been using soccer as an example throughout this book. In the sample you will read in *Writing Sample: Excerpt from Sample Student Expository Paper*, note that, rather than using her own experiences as the basis for the paper, the student uses historical examples and quotations from outside sources to support her thesis about teamwork and soccer. The sample paper below is an excerpt consisting of the introduction and first two body paragraphs of the paper.

Writing Sample: Excerpt from Sample Student Expository Paper

Over past decades, the sport of competitive soccer has taken the world by storm. In Europe, fanatic "football" fans make headlines for their passionate support of local teams. And in America, thousands of parents register children for youth soccer clubs each year. While many factors influence how successful any given team can be, by far the most important factor is teamwork. Using soccer as an example, this paper will explore what it takes to work successfully as a team, and how individual members can work together to achieve a common goal. It is clear that unity, confidence, and practice are critical components of successful teamwork within the sport of soccer.

A sense of unity and selflessness is, above all, critical to successful teamwork. A common saying regarding teamwork is that there is no "I" in the word "team," and this mindset is essential when it comes to soccer. As Mia Hamm, former professional player for the United States women's national soccer team once said, "I am a member of a team, and I rely on the team, I defer to it and sacrifice for it, because the team, not the individual, is the ultimate champion" (Hamm, 1994, para 3). In a sport where countries vie to compete for the famous World Cup, individual team members must put their country and their team first. For every soccer match played there may be up to eleven players on the field, and "a match may not start if either team has fewer than seven players" (FIFA, n.d., para 1). Relying on the team as a unit, rather than individual players, is the only way that a team can hope to win each game.

Team confidence is a second key to a soccer team's success. While a team may be talented, it is only if they have confidence in one another's abilities that winning becomes possible. Soccer history is full of stories of teams that beat the odds against them. In 1950, a ragtag American team played against England for the World Cup. According to an article in the *New York Times*, the English had invented the game of soccer "and were 3-1 favorites to win the tournament. The Americans were 500-1 long shots" (Longman, 2009, para. 6). However, the American team shocked the soccer world by winning the game with a 1-0 score. A more recent victory occurred when the English Liverpool club won a game against Italy's Juventus club. Player Steven Gerrard said of the win, "we were massive underdogs, so to beat them was fantastic" (Gerrard, 2005, para. 1). The above examples illustrate how confidence can benefit teamwork, resulting in successes that no one thought possible.

. . .

References

FIFA. (n.d.) Main website. Retrieved from http://www.fifa.com

Gerrard, S. (2005). Quotation. Retrieved from http://www.icelebz.com/quotes/steven_gerrard/

Hamm, M. (1994). Quotation. Retrieved from http://www.values.com/inspirational-sayings
-billboards/56-Passion

Longman, J. (2009, December 9). How a 'band of no-hopers' forged U.S. soccer's finest day.
The New York Times. Retrieved from http://www.nytimes.com/2009/12/10/sports/
soccer/10soccer.html?pagewanted=all&_r=0

Many of the essays you will be assigned in college courses call for an expository paper. When you are asked to write a brief informative paper, to respond to readings, to analyze or critique an issue, to compare and contrast theories or points of view, to explain a subject, or to explore causes and effects, you should use exposition to construct your essay. *Writing in Action: Sample Expository Paper Assignments* lists some sample expository writing assignments from actual courses. Note that each of these assignments asks you to share information, not to give your personal opinion of the issue. This characteristic should alert you that an expository response is needed.

Writing in Action: Sample Expository Paper Assignments

Key words and action verbs are underlined in the following examples:

- Identify two different cultures in the world and examine their traditions. Based on the behaviors, customs, and beliefs of each of the two cultures, discuss how personalities and identities are formed and shared within the two different cultures.
- Compose a two- to three-page essay using examples from two or more works read during the week. Reflect upon how literature reflects communities. You do *not* need resources *outside the course materials* for this essay; however, you *must* cite the works from the texts.
- A scholarly study of literature connects or compares works from different genres by using one literary element. This is your assignment: Find a way to connect or compare one literary work to two others.
- Compare and contrast the thought and philosophy of two philosophers mentioned in the text. Write an eight- to ten-page paper in which you address a brief history of the philosophers and discuss the view of each philosopher on metaphysics, epistemology, ethics, free will and/or determinism, personal identity, and the existence of God.
- Write an essay in which you summarize the stereotypes associated with the following groups and provide an explanation as to whether these stereotypes are positive, negative, or both: (1) politicians, (2) tattooed persons, (3) feminists, and (4) senior citizens.
- Write a five- to seven-page paper in which you discuss the advantages and disadvantages of bilingual education in elementary school classrooms.
- Write an eight-page reflective paper in which you demonstrate your understanding of the reading assignments and the implications of your new knowledge in this course. Integrate your readings and class discussions into your own work and life experience. Include explanations and examples from your previous experience. The purpose of the reflective paper is for you to culminate the learning achieved in the course by describing your understanding and application of knowledge in the philosophy of human conduct.

Tone and Language

Because expository writing deals with factual information, it should be devoid of emotion. Make sure to use formal language and to choose words that have clear, descriptive, nonemotional denotative meanings. This does not mean that your writing must be boring. Expository writing is about serious subjects, but it can also be rich with details, engage the reader, and be interesting to read.

Point of View

Expository writing should be objective and unbiased. Unlike personal or persuasive writing, your expository paper should not reveal your opinion or judgment of the information. Your task is simply to present it as fairly and accurately as you can. Expository writing focuses on the subject matter, so it generally uses a third-person point of view (*he, she, they, the subject, the author*). This focus can be lost when the point of view is shifted to the writer by using first person (*I, me, my, our*) or to the reader by using second person (*you, your*). However, when you write information that instructs someone how to perform a task, you may use a second-person viewpoint (*you*) or a viewpoint where the second person is understood—for example, an instruction directed to the reader, such as "[You] Open the folder."

Structure and Supporting Ideas

While expository papers generally follow the best practices laid out in Chapter 5, the sections below give additional details on how to structure a successful expository paper.

Thesis Statement

Remember that, like all well-written papers, expository papers must have a clear thesis. Make sure that your paper has a focus and a primary idea you want to get across to your readers. Here are some sample expository thesis statements and stronger, revised versions of each:

> **First draft thesis**: Many factors contributed to the rise of the suburbs, especially the development of the automobile.

> **Revised thesis**: The development of commuter trains and the automobile, along with the desire for people to be outside the city, contributed to the rise of the suburbs in America.

> **First draft thesis**: Cheese is primarily made by curdling milk and then by giving it time to age.

> **Revised thesis**: Cheese is made by a process of curdling milk, separating the curd from the whey, and drying and packing the curd, followed by an aging process. Various lengths of the aging process create different tastes, and even the scents in the room where the aging occurs can be used to impart flavor into the cheese.

> **First draft thesis**: According to Virginia Woolf, in *A Room of One's Own*, women must be granted the proper space to think and write.

> **Revised thesis**: Virginia Woolf's *A Room of One's Own* suggests that economic, social, and academic issues limit most women's ability to write in their time.

Paragraph Organization and Transitions

A well-written expository essay is organized in the sequence in which events occur, the order in which ideas should be considered, or the priority of the items discussed. When you use exposition to provide directions or to write instructions or procedures, it is imperative that you arrange the information in **chronological order**, the order in which tasks are performed, to ensure that the reader follows them correctly. Use of transitions is also critical in expository writing to ensure that readers do not get lost in your explanations and can follow along with your presentation of material. Signal word such as *first, after, next, last,* and *for example* are especially useful for this purpose. For example, if you are sharing information from an article you read in a magazine, and you have three main points to make, use signal words like these underlined terms to let readers know when you move from one main point to another: "The <u>first</u> point stated in the article is . . . . <u>Second</u>, the article suggests that . . . . <u>Finally</u>, the article recommends . . . ."

Short expository papers are read sequentially from beginning to end and do not usually contain headings, which are short phrases that separate and organize sections of the paper. However, with longer or more complex exposition, headings can be useful to help readers quickly and easily find information they need. In longer papers, use headings whenever you believe they will help readers stay on track with the information you are presenting.

Supporting Details

Finally, remember that when you present information, you must support your statements. Effective exposition supports ideas with facts, explanations, details, and examples to ensure that those ideas are clear to readers. When you state a main idea in your paper, make sure to develop that idea by following your statement with supporting ideas that are logically organized to make them clear and understandable. Unless a statement is a well-known fact, you must go on to explain that statement and support it in some way.

7.2 Conventions of Expository Writing

Exposition often incorporates *conventions*, or specific writing methods, that can help make your writing accurate, complete, clear, and focused. Use these conventions, as appropriate, in your expository writing to improve the effectiveness of your papers. Expository essays are generally written in the third person, unless your instructor specifically asks you to do otherwise. Expository essays are analytical essays and are asking for objective interpretations—that is, interpretations based on facts, details, or the language of texts you are asked to analyze.

Definition

Because information you present must be understandable to your readers, defining terms is particularly important in expository writing. **Defining terms** is a way to explain what a term means by labeling it and/or providing synonyms. In your expository writing, define any terms that you anticipate your readers might not understand. In a complex document, you might include these definitions in a vocabulary list or a glossary at the end of a document. For a shorter document, weave your definitions in the text in the paragraphs themselves, as we did above when we defined the word *conventions*. If you believe a term or a concept might still be misunderstood, even with the definition, include an example to show the reader how the term is used in a sentence.

Classification

Classification is a method of organizing information to help readers understand it; to classify, we group items in a category with other items that share similar characteristics and state the essential features of the item. For example, if you wanted to define the Microsoft PowerPoint™ software program, you might classify it by stating that it is a presentation development tool (the category) that contains background templates (essential feature) to allow users to create a presentation with a unified look (essential feature).

Description

Description is "painting pictures with words," which allows the reader to visualize the content of the essay. When we describe something, we list its characteristics and features or give an example to help illustrate it and create a mental picture of the item in the reader's mind. Description is often used with narration to help make information clear and vivid; however, it is also used in expository writing to clarify ideas and to help readers visualize an item clearly in their minds. By using description and including specific details that appeal to the reader's five senses and support or explain what we say, we can help the reader understand the information more clearly.

Svitlana Sokolva/Shutterstock.com

In choosing your words carefully, you can create an image for the reader to visualize.

7.3 Informative Writing

In some courses, particularly those in business and management, you will be asked to prepare reports or to share information about a project. This kind of a report would require you to use **informative writing**, a type of expository writing that provides the reader with facts about a particular topic, such as a description of how something works.

The Purpose of Informative Writing

Informative writing is meant to educate the reader and answer the questions "how" or "why" about the given topic. This type of writing usually involves more than one subject and concerns complex issues that must be described and discussed in detail. Informative reports may require that you perform research and then share your research findings in the report. In general, informative writing does not include persuasive elements. However, some reports, such as recommendation reports and proposals, are persuasive in nature. Many reports are informative and are designed to provide information to help organizational decision making. These informative reports should be written as expository documents.

Understanding Informative Writing

You can recognize an informative writing assignment because the assignment will ask you to describe the details of a topic or explain to the reader how a process works, such as in the example below:

> *Example*: Describe in detail the process of hydraulic fracturing, or "fracking," and its effect on groundwater. Remember to include factual information about the process as well as accurate data about the effect on groundwater.

Notice that the assignment does not ask you to persuade or advise the reader, but to provide factual details only. This is a sign that you will need to write an informative report to answer the prompt.

Structure of Informative Papers

Informative writing can be of any length, from one or two pages to several hundred pages. Keep in mind that not all types of informative papers will require a formal thesis. For example, if you were to write a paper describing how to build a piece of furniture, your opening paragraph would not need to include a thesis. Such a paper does not require you to make a claim or persuade the reader, but to explain the steps in a process.

However, there are some types of informative papers that will require a thesis. Usually, this will be a combination paper, such as an informative analysis paper or an informative persuasive paper. These types of papers ask you to give factual details supported by primary or secondary research, and then to analyze those details or persuade the reader to accept your interpretation of the factual information.

7.4 Comparison and Contrast Writing

A comparison-and-contrast paper examines both similarities and differences in the same paper. Comparison and contrast are two sides of the same coin. When you compare subjects, you show how they are alike; when you contrast them, you show how they are different. In effective comparison-and-contrast papers, though, one or the other is generally the focus and has more emphasis.

The Purpose of Comparison-and-Contrast Writing

Comparison and contrast are useful in helping readers understand issues. They can also be helpful in evaluating options, narrowing down choices, and making decisions. Often without realizing it, we use these patterns every day, for decisions small and large. When we decide whether we want to have a blueberry muffin or an apple for breakfast, choose whether to watch the news or a reality show on television, select a brand of soda, or determine which university to attend to complete our college degree, we are using comparison and contrast and making decisions from among various alternatives. We may not consciously weigh all the pros and cons of each alternative before making the decision; however, some factors usually sway our decision one way or the other. For example, we may decide to have the muffin on the basis of taste or select the apple based on calorie count.

Understanding Comparison-and-Contrast Writing

You can recognize a comparison-and-contrast assignment because the assignment will ask you to examine two or more issues. It may not specifically use the words *compare* or *contrast*. Instead, it may ask you to discuss similarities and differences, advantages and disadvantages, pros and cons, or the relative merits of one subject over another. It might also use comparative words as in the following comparative assignment:

pathdoc/Shutterstock.com

Comparing and contrasting ideas can help your reader understand a complex issue.

> *Example*: Your manager is considering the purchase of a new printer for the office and has asked you to prepare a report that discusses the features of available printers that will help her determine which brand and model would be the most cost effective to purchase.

The word *most* is the comparative word that gives you the clue that a comparison-and-contrast paper is required.

To use comparison and contrast, the subjects you choose must have some similarities, or comparison is difficult, if not impossible. You have probably heard the expression, "You can't compare them; it is like comparing apples and oranges." Actually, this saying is untrue; you can compare apples and oranges because they have some common features. They are both edible, they are both fruits, and they are both juicy. It would be much more difficult to compare apples and bicycles or oranges and rubber bands.

Let us look at the elements of effective comparison and contrast and discuss how to incorporate them in any comparison-and-contrast papers you write.

Find Commonalities and Differences

An expository comparison-and-contrast paper simply presents and examines factors or issues to help the reader make his or her own decision about an issue. When you compare and/or contrast, your job is to consciously think about the factors that might influence a decision, to discuss these factors, and to weigh them or comment on them in the paper. In a comparison-and-contrast paper, you do not necessarily make the decision yourself or attempt to influence the reader one way or the other. If you do so, your paper will be a combination of expository and persuasive writing.

You might begin the prewriting process of your comparison-and-contrast paper by creating a list or a table of the features the subjects have in common and the features they have that are different. For example, with our printer comparison above, you might ask yourself: What printers are available? What features do the available printers have in common? What are the major differences among them? You might consider features such as the cost of the toner cartridge, the paper size accepted, the printing speed, the printing volume or capacity, and the availability of a preview screen or of tech support. Table 7.1 illustrates a table constructed to show the similarities and differences in the printers that were researched.

Table 7.1: Example of a comparison-and-contrast table

	Printer A	Printer B	Printer C	Printer D
Purchase Price	$199	$150	$299	$350
Basic Features				
Type of printer	Laser	Laser	Laser	Laser
Color or monochrome	Monochrome	Monochrome	Monochrome	Monochrome
Connection	USB, Ethernet	USB, Ethernet, wireless	USB, parallel, Ethernet	USB, parallel, serial, Ethernet
Max. paper size	Legal	Legal	Legal	Letter
Speed and Capacity				
Rated speed	30 pp. per min	23 pp. per min	25 pp. per min	33 pp. per min
Print volume	25,000 pp. per month	15,000 pp. per month	11,000 pp. per month	25,000 pp. per month
Paper capacity	300 sheets	250 sheets	150 sheets	200 sheets
Special Features				
Duplexing	Yes	No	No	Yes
LCD preview screen	No	Yes	No	Yes
Cost per Page	2.7¢	1.8¢	2.8¢	1.6¢
Cost of Toner and Number of Prints	$62 2,300 pp.	$46 2,600 pp.	$55 2,000 pp.	$56 3,500 pp.
Tech Support	With purchase of service pkg. ($150/year)	Toll-free number weekdays only 8–5 EST	Toll-free number available 24/7	With purchase of service pkg. ($99/year)

Once you have created your list or table of similarities and differences, you must examine the lists and choose a basis for comparison. Our printers, for example, have many features, but not all of them will be important or appropriate for your paper. Your assignment asks you to focus on which printer would be the most cost effective. A feature such as the availability of a preview screen, for example, may not be important for a decision based on cost effectiveness.

The basis of comparison that you decide to discuss in your paper will be the similarities and/or differences among the printers that are important to the purchase decision. In other words, which printer features must be considered if you are making the decision based on cost effectiveness? If the available printers are very similar, you might briefly mention the common features they share and focus your paper on exploring the contrasts in more depth. On the other hand, if subjects are very different, the similarities might be the most interesting and the most important to explore.

One way to approach the basis of comparison is to first set some criteria for that comparison. Your assignment asks you to determine cost effectiveness, so you know that the initial price of the printers is an important criterion. Because printers can range in cost from below $100 to more than $1,000, you might decide to use printers under $400 as a basis for comparison, as we did in our example. If so, make sure to explain your reason for this choice in your paper.

Let us say that you work for a law firm, and you know that your company must be able to print on both letter-sized and legal-sized paper. It would probably not be cost effective to buy a second printer just for the legal-sized documents, so a printer that can print on both letter- and legal-sized paper will be an important criterion. Use issues such as these to narrow down the features of the items you are comparing into the ones you think will be most important when making the purchase decision. To help you construct your paper, you might list, highlight, or circle the features on the printed material from your research that you intend to compare and contrast in your paper.

Structure of Comparison-and-Contrast Papers

Like all well-written papers, your comparison-and-contrast paper should have a clear and focused thesis statement. Your thesis statement should be an answer to a meaningful interpretive question you have about a text, experiment, policy, or other scenario. Write down this thesis statement as a tentative idea of your primary point. In our printer example, the thesis statement was suggested in the assignment itself when it asked you to focus on cost effectiveness. Some comparison-and-contrast expository papers are also combination papers that ask you to formulate an argument toward the end of the paper after you have carefully assessed the main features of each primary concept.

Select an Organizational Arrangement

Comparison-and-contrast papers are most often arranged in one of two different ways: a block arrangement or a point-by-point arrangement. A **block arrangement** mentions all the features about one subject before it moves on to another subject. Let us go back to our printer example and imagine that you found three printers that meet the criteria you developed. A block arrangement outline for a discussion of the features of these three printers might look something like Figure 7.1. Notice that all the features for printer A that you selected for your basis of comparison are discussed before you discuss printers B and C. Remember that all features you mentioned regarding printer A must also be mentioned when you construct the sections of the paper relating to printers B and C.

Figure 7.1: Example of a block arrangement

I. Introduction

II. Printer A
   A. Purchase Price
   B. Speed and Capacity
   C. Cost per Page
   D. Cost of Toner and Number of Prints
   E. Tech Support

III. Printer B
   A. Purchase Price
   B. Speed and Capacity
   C. Cost per Page
   D. Cost of Toner and Number of Prints
   E. Tech Support

IV. Printer C
   A. Purchase Price
   B. Speed and Capacity
   C. Cost per Page
   D. Cost of Toner and Number of Prints
   E. Tech Support

V. Conclusion

A second method of arranging a comparison-and-contrast paper is called the **point-by-point arrangement**. When you compare or contrast subjects point by point, you choose one feature at a time and alternate between the subjects when discussing that feature. For example, you might take the feature of a low cost per page. You might first explain that the cost per page is based on the cost of the printer cartridge and the number of pages printed. Then, you would discuss the cost per page for printer A, printer B, and printer C. After you have discussed this feature as it relates to all three printers, you would then move on to the second feature you want to compare, printing on both letter- and legal-sized paper, and compare this feature on printers A, B, and C. Continue this way until you have compared and contrasted each feature you outlined in your thesis statement. Review Figure 7.2 to see how a paper with a point-by-point arrangement would be constructed.

Figure 7.2: Example of a point-by-point arrangement

I. Introduction

II. First Difference: Purchase Price
    A. Printer A
    B. Printer B
    C. Printer C

III. Second Difference: Speed and Capacity
    A. Printer A
    B. Printer B
    C. Printer C

IV. Third Difference: Cost per Page
    A. Printer A
    B. Printer B
    C. Printer C

V. Fourth Difference: Cost of Toner and Number of Prints
    A. Printer A
    B. Printer B
    C. Printer C

VI. Fifth Difference: Tech Support
    A. Printer A
    B. Printer B
    C. Printer C

VII. Conclusion

The point-by-point arrangement is preferable if your paper is lengthy or if the subject matter is complex. With lengthy or complex subjects, a point-by-point comparison makes it less likely that your readers will become lost or confused during the comparisons and contrasts.

Every writing situation is different, and you may see some professional essays that combine comparison and contrast in the same paper. You may choose this combination approach yourself if you have a complex issue to discuss. However, don't try to combine the patterns unless you are extremely careful not to confuse yourself or your readers with this combined approach. You would need to use very careful signal words and transitional sentences to make the format of your paper—and your reasons for structuring it in this way—clear.

Make the Comparison or Contrast Apparent to Readers

When you are comparing or contrasting items, do not just list the features of one item and then the features of another. Instead, show how the items are related to one another. Remember to use transitions, which we discussed in Chapter 5, to indicate the relationship among items. See how much easier the information is to understand and how much better the writing flows in the second example below when transitions are inserted to show the relationships among the various printers:

> *Poor example*: Printer A prints 30 pages per minute and 25,000 pages per month. Printer B prints 23 pages per minute and 15,000 pages per month. Printer C prints 25 pages per minute and 11,000 pages per month. Printer D prints 30 pages per minute and 25,000 pages per month.

Better example: Both Printers A and D print 30 pages per minute and produce 25,000 pages per month. By contrast, printer B prints only 23 pages per minute and 15,000 pages per month, while printer C prints a little faster at 25 pages per minute but produces the fewest prints at only 11,000 pages per month.

Table 7.2 shows a list of transitions that indicate similarity (comparison) and difference (contrast).

Table 7.2: Signal words that indicate similar or different items

Words that show similarity/comparison	like, likewise, similar, similarly, in the same way, just as, for example, such, at the same time, along these lines, by analogy, comparably, both, all, accordingly, in comparison, analogous, comparable
Words that show difference/contrast	however, unlike, on the other hand, but, yet, still, nor, though, while, nevertheless, nonetheless, on the contrary, in contrast, by contrast, although, albeit, instead, rather, conversely, otherwise, in spite of, alternately, alternatively, more than, most, fewer than, fewest

The following link contains an excellent example of a comparison-and-contrast essay. As you read this essay, see if you can identify the elements of an effective comparison-and-contrast essay that we have discussed in this chapter: http://www.hillsdale.edu/news /imprimis/archive/issue.asp?year=2009&month=02.

7.5 Cause-and-Effect Writing

Another pattern of exposition that you may be required to use in your college writing is a **cause-and-effect paper**, which explores the relationship between underlying factors and influences and their consequences. Cause-and-effect writing allows us to identify or to speculate about the reasons why something happened, to understand the results of a particular action, or both. The cause is the action that made the situation occur, and the effect is the result of that action. Cause-and-effect relationships, however, are rarely that simple.

The Purpose of Cause-and-Effect Writing

Cause-and-effect writing explores, attempts to explain, or investigates probable causes and probable effects. It does not attempt to prove anything; you may explore various causes, or the degree to which various causes led to something. If your paper argues for a particular point of view and attempts to convince readers that your viewpoint is correct, you have moved from expository writing to persuasive writing. Note that an assignment may be a combination paper that asks you to explore causes and effects and then to develop an interpretation of the primary causes toward the end of the paper—this would mean that you develop an argument after addressing a variety of causes and effects.

Thus, cause-and-effect writing is often used as a preface to persuasive and argumentative writing. Before you can persuade someone to accept your point of view or convince him or her to take some action you recommend, you must first give them reasons why they should do so. Just as an attorney must argue in court and provide evidence to support that argument to attempt to prove that someone committed a crime, you must also make a strong and compelling argument and provide sufficient evidence when you attempt to prove a cause-and-effect relationship between two issues.

Mastering the skills of this pattern of exposition is essential for effective persuasive writing. Click on the link below and read the sample essay that discusses U.S. health care (*A Prescription for American Health Care*, by John Goodman):

https://imprimis.hillsdale.edu/a-prescription-for-american-health-care/

Can you identify the section of the essay that is written using the cause-and-effect pattern and the point at which the author switches to persuasive writing?

ConstantinosZ/Shutterstock.com

A cause-and-effect pattern may be used to support a persuasive paper arguing that smoking causes lung cancer.

Understanding Cause-and-Effect Writing

Any essay that asks you to investigate, illuminate, or assess contributory causes of some particular effect qualifies as a cause-and-effect paper. A paper may ask you to identify the particular causes leading up to a historical event. A different assignment may ask you to discuss and evaluate the factors that contributed to a particular environmental change. A more typical assignment for an English course may ask you to identify the reasons for a particular change in a character.

Causal Analysis

Often you will observe a problem or situation, and you will want to determine its cause or causes. Typically, there may be several underlying causes to a problem, and if you write an essay about cause and effect, you will decide what the main causes are that contribute to the scenario you are examining. Let us say, for example, that you notice the grass in your backyard is turning brown, and you want to know why. Finding causes is similar to creating links in a chain. If you can connect one link in the chain to the next link and the next and the next, eventually you will have a fairly strong chain (and a fairly clear picture of the cause of a problem). In fact, looking for causes is often referred to as creating a **causal chain** (Figure 7.3). Follow these steps to create this causal chain:

1. Begin with the observed effect: the brown grass.
2. Speculate on possible factors that might have caused the problem.
3. Assess the probability of each of these possibilities or investigate them one by one to attempt to eliminate them.
4. Conclude with the probable cause.

Figure 7.3: A causal chain

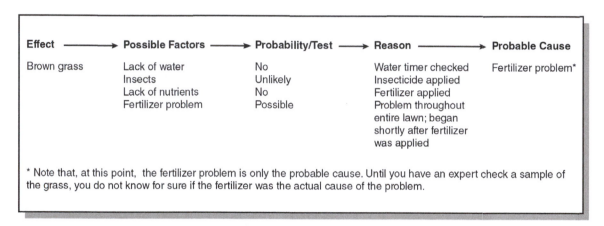

Effect ⟶	Possible Factors ⟶	Probability/Test ⟶	Reason ⟶	Probable Cause
Brown grass	Lack of water	No	Water timer checked	Fertilizer problem*
	Insects	Unlikely	Insecticide applied	
	Lack of nutrients	No	Fertilizer applied	
	Fertilizer problem	Possible	Problem throughout entire lawn; began shortly after fertilizer was applied	

* Note that, at this point, the fertilizer problem is only the probable cause. Until you have an expert check a sample of the grass, you do not know for sure if the fertilizer was the actual cause of the problem.

To elaborate on the example of the suburbs mentioned earlier in the chapter, another possible causal analysis assignment could ask you to consider why suburbs proliferated in America. In the 1910s, the development of streetcar lines enabled people to move out of cities. In the 1920s, rapid expansion of automobile use and availability combined with the decentralization of manufacturing (manufacturers moved out of cities to cheaper areas where they could build bigger plants) contributed to the development of the suburbs. After World War II, the biggest suburban expansion in the United States was due to consumer demand, marriages, and the baby boom.

Forms of Cause-and-Effect Relationships

You can recognize cause-and-effect writing assignments because they will ask you to discuss or explain the reasons why something occurred or contain the key words/phrases *if . . . then, as a result of . . . , as a consequence of . . . , the reasons for . . . , therefore,* or *because.* Following is a link to a professional cause-and-effect essay that uses one of the forms of cause-and-effect relationships listed in Table 7.3: http://faculty.ucc.edu/english-chewning /catton.htm. Can you identify the relationship the writer employs?

Table 7.3: Types of Cause-and-Effect Relationships

Cause-and-Effect Relationship	Example
Single cause with multiple effects	*Single cause*: Walmart opens a superstore in a community. *Multiple effects*: new jobs, more selection and convenience for shoppers, increased sales tax revenue for community, loss of business for local stores, loss of jobs with competitors, and loss of parking revenue for city downtown area
Single effect with multiple causes	*Single effect*: You own a local restaurant, and business is slow lately. *Multiple causes*: families trying to save money by eating at home, people want more nutritious food choices than you offer, outside family activities make it too difficult for families to eat together at the same time, an *E. coli* health problem at another restaurant has kept them away from restaurants, and a new restaurant opened down the street
Multiple causes and multiple effects	*Multiple causes*: historical disputes among people in the Middle East, political differences, religious differences, outside interference by other nations, fringe political groups, changing economic conditions, disputes over land and natural resources *Multiple effects*: Palestinian and Israeli conflict, political issues in Middle East countries, growth of militarism, growth in power and personal wealth of the elite, rise in Islamic militancy, global struggle to control access to oil reserves
Series of events	The clearest example of a series of events is the poem that Benjamin Franklin made famous by placing it in his book *Poor Richard's Almanac*, which shows that a seemingly minor event can lead to significant consequences: *"For Want of a Nail"* For want of a nail the shoe was lost. For want of a shoe the horse was lost. For want of a horse the rider was lost. For want of a rider the battle was lost. For want of a battle the kingdom was lost. And all for the want of a horseshoe nail. (Hoyt & Roberts, 2009)

When you write a cause-and-effect paper, you are attempting to understand the relationship between decision, actions, and events and their causes and effects. It is important to recognize, however, that simply because two events occurred near each other in time, one did not necessarily cause the other.

For instance, perhaps a traveler returned from an airplane flight across country and, a few days later, came down with the flu. If that traveler assumes, without any evidence, that the airplane flight caused her flu, she would be guilty of an error known as the *post hoc ergo propter hoc* fallacy. The term ***post hoc ergo propter hoc*** is a Latin phrase that means "after this therefore because of this," and a *fallacy* is a logical error or a mistake in reasoning. If two events happen next to each other in time, we cannot simply assume that because one event happened after another, the first event was the cause of the second. The traveler might speculate that the flu could have been caused by a bug she picked up on the flight, but it might also have been a coincidence that the flight and the flu occurred near each other in time.

Structure of Cause-and-Effect Papers

Like a comparison-and-contrast paper, cause-and-effect writing can be structured in one of two ways. After constructing your introduction, the first option is to begin the body of the paper with causes, to discuss them thoroughly, and then move on to discussing effects. For more complex situations, you will likely have to choose a few main causes and just a few of the most significant effects. A second option is to discuss a cause and its effects thoroughly and then move on to other causes and other effects, if necessary. This method may only work if the causes are very separate from one another—but if the causes are directly linked to one another, it will likely be more effective to discuss the entire set of causes first—the entire causal chain—before moving on to the significant effects.

7.6 Analytical Writing

Another common type of expository writing assignment you will encounter in your college courses is that of the **analytical paper**, which asks you to respond to material you have read and to provide insight into the meaning of that material. When we analyze something, we break it into its component parts in an attempt to understand it more thoroughly.

The Purpose of Analytical Writing

In your courses, you may be asked to interpret a piece of literature, a philosophical perspective, or a theory. Interpretive writing does not merely summarize events, and it does not judge them. It focuses on helping readers understand the meaning and analyzing how the writer conveyed that meaning. If you are asked to evaluate ideas and then judge, argue, or defend your interpretation, your paper will be a combination of expository and persuasive writing. In an analytical paper that is expository but not persuasive, you will simply analyze and explain issues and support your interpretation with details and specific examples from the material itself.

Analytical papers are called by many different names. In a process analysis or process explanation paper, for instance, you are asked to analyze a task or operation that moves through a series of steps. The process might be a physical one such as the writing process, a mental one such as the decision-making process, a mechanical one such as the process for canning fruit, or a natural process such as breathing. Process explanation papers require you to understand and communicate the main components of a process usually in sequential, time order, and to understand the logical connections among the various elements of the process.

Understanding Analytical Writing

Another type of analytical paper is a **mechanism description** or analysis. In this type of paper, you break a simple or complex piece of equipment into its component parts, describe those parts, and attempt to show how it works. People write mechanism descriptions about objects as simple as a ballpoint pen or as complex as a rocket engine. An example of this might be found in an owner's manual for an appliance. You likely would not have to write this kind of paper, but if you did, it would probably be for a science class that is asking you to describe a scientific mechanism.

In your college courses, you might also be asked to construct **problem–solution papers**. These analytical papers define a problem, suggest alternative solutions to the problem, and discuss each potential solution. Like many other expository papers, problem–solution papers often form the foundation for persuasive writing. After the problem is identified and alternatives discussed, the writer may then make a proposal or structure a persuasive report to recommend a particular solution be adopted. This kind of paper might be written for a public policy course in which you would write a proposal on some sort of current policy or for advocating the adoption of a new policy.

Structure of Analytical Papers

All the analytical papers we have discussed incorporate the characteristics outlined earlier in this chapter for expository papers. They have as their common goal to share information with readers. They also deal with factual information and share this information, in an objective manner, with readers. As you read the sample analytical essay written by an actual student below, please pay particular attention to the structure of the essay and the ways in which the main idea is developed.

Writing Sample: Student Essay
Science Fiction in Young Adult Literature

A hook that directly pertains to the subject

Appropriate contextualization of Science Fiction

An arguable topic sentence that directly relates to the thesis

Introduces the author and text

A two-sentence thesis. The last part of the second sentence conveys the "so what?" or explanation of why the Science Fiction genre may be important, for it is "much like the transition out of adolescence and into adulthood."

As Young Adult literature moved into the latter half of the twentieth century, it began to incorporate a litany of other genres, from the familiar didactic and adventure stories, to fantasy and romance. Among these, the genre of Science Fiction is well suited to address the changing roles of humans in a more universal context experienced during the mid-twentieth century. In her book *A Wrinkle in Time,* Madeline L'Engle successfully employs Science Fiction within the Young Adult genre, and uses it to address the concerns of a changing generation of Young Adult readers. Assuming that the purpose of Young Adult literature is not solely to entertain, but to educate, the genre of Science Fiction is particularly appropriate for addressing a young audience growing up in a world of change. It removes the protagonists from a familiar world and places them in a larger context in which they must encounter ideas and circumstances greater than themselves, much like the transition out of adolescence and into adulthood.

L'Engle uses Science Fiction to move the didactic coming of age story out of a familiar world. L'Engle wrote in a generation of rapid and destabilizing changes; things previously considered science fantasy were becoming modern day realities. Where a previous generation may have some trouble accepting such "facts" as space travel, a younger, more readily shaped youth would potentially not

(continued)

This section of the essay presents the problem or question the essay is trying to answer, and gives a potential answer to that question—that the Science Fiction genre offers a sense of "adolescent bewilderment."

only accept these ideas as plausible, but expand upon them until they were possible. What is truly striking about *A Wrinkle in Time* is how applicable it is, not only to its contemporary generation of Young Adults, but to consecutive ones as well. In 1962, the year in which L'Engle's book was published, it was possible for adolescents to get an idea of what was happening in a world outside their own through radio and television. This fact certainly holds true today, though on an even grander scale. However, within the confines of school and family, it is difficult to get an accurate idea of life outside of one's own sphere, and further to consider that that life is much more complex than what one is used to. The challenge, then, is to illustrate a sense of adolescent bewilderment in a less familiar way. In other words, how best can the Young Adult reader be removed from the familiar, or at least a world that is seemingly so, and confronted with one that is not? The answer: through the imaginative, but not entirely unrealistic, realm of Science Fiction. Science Fiction during the 1960s was able to address a youth experiencing a growth in scientific discovery and questioning of human beings' place in the Universe. As L'Engle herself notes, "My entire life has been full of change. We've gone from riding a horse to traveling in space all in one lifetime" (1982). Space is perhaps the final frontier which we accept exists, but which we collectively do not understand. This mysteriousness makes space a perfect arena in which to set a story about differences and the unknown. It prompts us to ask the big questions, such as, "Is there life out there aside from what we know here on earth?" and "What is our place within such a large universe?" The transition from the familiarity of childhood into adolescence, and again from adolescence into adulthood prompts much the same questions for a young adult reader.

Direct citation is used as evidence to support the claim of the paragraph

This topic sentence adds another layer of complexity by claiming that the novel is imaginative but has realistic elements.

Though L'Engle's story certainly delves into a world of imagination, it is still grounded in reality. Meg's transformation is not unbelievable; it is relatable at its core, which makes it appealing to young adults. Meg is an outcast; she is plain and awkward, and has trouble maturing with the rest of her peers. Young adult readers can sympathize with these issues, and through this identification with Meg, they are able to experience her growth and rebirth. At the beginning of *A Wrinkle in Time,* Meg wonders why she cannot be like everyone else. L'Engle answers this question by literally creating a world in which all beings are alike. The darkness pervading this world is a manifestation of physical and social conformity; those who give in to the darkness are stripped of their individuality. As Charles Wallace, under the influence of IT, explains, "On Camazotz we are all happy because we are all alike. Differences create problems. You know that's the reason you're not happy at school. Because you're different" (L'Engle, 1962, p. 131). Meg has been shown to struggle with her differences throughout the book, and it is not until she accepts these differences that she can become an effective member of the group. Though her awareness of this comes gradually, Meg's experience on the strange, dystopian world of Camazotz prompts her to the realization that "Maybe [she doesn't] like being different, but [she doesn't] want to be like everybody else, either" (L'Engle, 1962, p. 131). This realization allows Meg to grow and understand that perhaps being like everyone else will not make her as happy as she previously assumed back on Earth. The book specifically identifies historical figures that have stood up in the face of conformity, who question rather than blindly accept. Those who struggle against society's norms, against IT, are considered to be the light against the darkness of conformity. Meg is shown throughout the book to be different from those around her, and these differences are what make her such an important part of the defense against the universal attack on individuality by IT.

A multi-sentence analysis of the last few quotes in this paragraph. It elaborates on the concept of conformity in the novel and relates this to Meg's character.

(continued)

Writing Sample: Student Essay
Science Fiction in Young Adult Literature **(continued)**

This topic sentence could take a clearer position in relation to the thesis.

At the onset of the story, Meg falls very much into the second stage of psychologist Otto Rank's stages of adolescent development: she is doing poorly in school and rebelling against authority figures, such as her teachers and her principal, Mr. Jenkins. Meg is unable to conform to her surrounding society, but at the same time is also unable to form an effective identity. For her to become a contributing member of society as an adult, it is essential that Meg pass into Rank's third stage, that of the hero. Through the events on her journey to rescue her father from the evil IT on Camazotz, Meg learns the difference between rebelling ineffectively and affecting change within society. Her own values of love and a newly found acceptance of not only her own, but others' differences, allow her to become a force for progress and social change. Her defeat of IT's control over her brother, Charles Wallace, gives us an example of how resistance of authority, when used in the right way, can be effective. Meg's resistance to authority in school on Earth was only undermining her ability to function effectively in society rather than enhancing it. However, her resistance of IT's control is shown to be absolutely essential in preserving the good kind of society that we as readers want Meg, and ourselves, to be a part of. We want Meg to resist, and what is more, Meg needs to resist. It is necessary for Meg to push such boundaries in order for her to understand her own individual freedoms and limitations before she enters the adult world. Individuality is important within a context of interdependency. Meg, regardless of an acceptance of her differences, would not have been able to come to the conclusion she does without working with, and within, a certain society. She gives and receives help between many of the other characters, and this learning to work within will transfer to her life back on Earth. Rather than continuing to act up in school, to be an outsider, Meg can now see how she functions as a part of a larger whole, and will work within that whole to affect change and progress.

These sentences analyze the relationship between independence and a development of a sense of self as part of a society. Notice that each sentence adds something new to this discussion.

This topic sentence could be strengthened by explaining how adolescence is cast "into a much larger universe." Why is this important to mention?

L'Engle takes the realistic world of fourteen-year-old Meg, a world fraught with the adversities of high school and adolescence, and casts it into a much larger universe. By placing Meg's journey of growth in a Science Fiction setting, L'Engle allows Meg to come to terms with her place not only in her own world, that of her family and peers, but within a more universal context as well. According to author William Sleator, "the richer a person's fantasy life, the better s/he is able to deal with real life. Imaginative literature is not only entertainment; it stimulates and exercises the reader's imagination and improves fantasy skills, making him/her better able to cope with frustrating situations in the real world" (1988, p. 4). The idea is, then, that through experiencing other worlds and encountering perhaps less plausible situations through reading Science Fiction, Young Adults learn the skills which better allow them to address, understand, and cope with unfamiliar situations in their own lives. For Meg in *A Wrinkle in Time*, this proves to be ultimately true. We can surmise that had Meg never journeyed to Camazotz, she may never have encountered such a fantastic world which would allow her to question and discover her own place in the universe. She would not have been tested and ultimately led to the rebirth necessary for her transition into adulthood. L'Engle creates a story that is new and different, and that challenges what we know with important questions. Perhaps this is why her novel was both rejected 26 times before being published, and then went on to win the 1963 Newbery Medal for the most distinguished contribution to American literature for children. This mixed reception of the book seems fitting, for it questions what we know, which can be hard to accept, but through this questioning, opens up the possibilities of an entirely new and imaginative future.

A "so what?" sentence that indicates a practical application of this novel.

Shows a complex understanding of the novel, and indicates one aspect of the novel's significance.

(continued)

Writing Sample: Student Essay
Science Fiction in Young Adult Literature **(continued)**

References

L'Engle, M. (1962). *A wrinkle in time.* New York, NY: Dell.

L'Engle, M. (1982). "Subject to change without notice." *Theory into Practice,(21)*4, Children's Literature (Autumn, 1982). Abingdon, VA: Taylor& Francis.

Sleator, W. (1988). *What is it about science fiction? ALAN Review (15)*2. Retrieved from http:// go.galegroup.comlpsli.do?&id=GALE% 7CHI420078308&v=2.1 &u=&it=r&p=LitRC&sw=w>

Chapter Summary

Exposition, or expository writing, is one of the most common types of writing you will encounter in your college classes and in the workplace. When we write expository papers, we share information with readers. Exposition can have many purposes—to inform readers about a topic, to clarify or explain a concept or idea, to define terms, to analyze a subject or text, to instruct readers, to describe an item, to explore ideas, or to interpret a subject so that it is understandable to readers.

Because effective exposition requires that readers understand the information you present, it is imperative that your writing be accurate, complete, clear, and focused. To accomplish these goals, exposition uses formal language and employs words that have clear, descriptive, nonemotional denotative meanings. It also often incorporates specific writing conventions such as definition, classification, and description to ensure that readers understand the information presented.

A wide range and variety of different types of academic and professional papers fall into the category of expository writing, including essays, informative reports, reflective papers, and interpretive papers. Many discussion-post responses also require a response that is written in an expository manner. Some types of exposition follow prescribed patterns that have their own specific elements or approaches. Comparison-and-contrast, cause-and-effect, and analytical papers are categories of exposition that require specific formats and structures—and these papers are frequently reflective papers (rather than simply informing readers of a topic, they tend to ask students to analyze and synthesize material). Although exposition encompasses a broad field of many types of papers, the basic principles of this type of writing are provided in this chapter. Mastering the essentials of exposition we have discussed here will give you the tools you need to excel at many of your writing tasks both in college and in your present or future career.

Key Terms

analytical paper A paper in which a writer offers an interpretation of a text, event, circumstance, or other objects of analysis.

block arrangement A type of organizational arrangement that mentions all the features about one subject before it moves on to another subject.

causal chain A type of analysis that perceives a sequence of events in which one event causes the next.

cause-and-effect paper Assesses the factors that led to a particular effect.

chronological order A type of organization that presents tasks in the order in which they are performed and information in the order in which it occurred in time, usually from earliest to latest.

classification A method of organizing information by grouping items into categories with other items that share similar characteristics.

comparison-and-contrast paper A type of expository paper that assesses the main similarities and differences between two or more subjects.

defining terms Explaining what a term means by labeling it and/or providing synonyms.

description Characterizing or giving qualities in order to make something vivid to the reader.

informative writing A type of expository writing that provides the reader with facts about a particular topic, such as a description of how something works.

mechanism description A type of analytical paper in which one breaks a simple or complex piece of equipment into its component parts, describes those parts, and attempts to show how it works.

point-by-point arrangement A method of arranging a comparison-and-contrast paper in which one compares or contrasts subjects point by point, choosing one feature at a time and alternating between the subjects when discussing that feature.

post hoc ergo propter hoc A Latin phrase meaning "after this therefore because of this."

problem–solution paper A type of analytical paper in which the author defines a problem, suggests alternative solutions to the problem, and discusses each potential solution.

Revising, Editing, and Proofreading

8

Supamotion/Shutterstock.com

Learning Objectives

After reading this chapter, you should be able to do the following:

1. Practice revising your paper.

2. Examine your paper for focus, organization, and completion.

3. Distinguish between revision and editing.

4. Understand language choice concepts such as tone, genre, denotation/connotation, and synonyms.

5. Utilize editing strategies to check for clarity and conciseness, as well as proofreading and format-checking strategies.

My first draft usually has only a few elements worth keeping.

I have to find what those are and build from them and throw out what doesn't work, or what simply is not alive.

—Susan Sontag

From *Essentials of College Writing: Contemporary Applications, 2/E* by Christine M. Connell and Kathy Sole. © 2013 Bridgepoint Education.

Writing is more akin to running a marathon than a sprint: Pacing yourself for a longer run that has a varying terrain is the best mental approach to writing. In writing an essay, your terrain consists not only of the prewriting process discussed in Chapter 4 but also the revising, editing, and proofreading stages. When a writer tries to sprint through one or more of these stages rather than taking the leisurely marathon route, the final writing product suffers. Depending on the length of the assignment and the amount of time given to complete it, revising, editing, and proofreading should occur over the course of many days, if not weeks. Like marathon running, writing requires conditioning and patience: The more a writer conditions and paces herself, the easier it is to produce a successful final draft.

8.1 The First Draft

Always assume that you will need to spend a lot of time revising your papers. Plan to set aside the required time and avoid procrastination. All of the prewriting materials you have composed, such as an outline or a mind map, will assist you in generating the first draft of your paper. Reread those drafting materials several times to gain a sense of how to respond to a particular writing prompt and how to best organize your ideas. Look for the tentative thesis, the synthesis of ideas you wrote out while brainstorming. Refer to the tentative outline to structure the order of main points and evidence that might be used. Note main ideas and concepts that you arrived at while brainstorming.

Getting Content Down on Paper

On writing a first draft, Irish author Frank O'Connor states, "I write any sort of rubbish which will cover the main outlines of the story, then I can begin to see it (Winokur, 1990, p. 243). Joyce Cary, another Irish writer, shares his method of drafting this way: "I may start anywhere, in the middle or at the end. I may go from the end to the beginning in the same day, and then from the beginning to the middle" (Winokur, 1990, p. 244).

When you are creating the first draft, keep writing until you have said everything you want to say about a certain point. Then move on to another point and write down everything you want to say about that point. Try not to stop writing to correct mistakes, check a word, find a different word, or otherwise edit your work. In his best selling book, *Way of the Peaceful Warrior*, author Dan Millman writes, "There is a saying: 'When you sit, sit; when you stand, stand; whatever you do, don't wobble' . . ." (Millman, 1984, p. 133). This saying can be adapted to writing: "When you write, write; when you edit, edit; whatever you do, do not wobble." Just keep writing.

If you get stuck while you are drafting and are not sure what to say, you have several options:

- Skip over the difficult part, leave a blank space, and keep going.
- Write anything, no matter how silly it sounds.
- Jot down new ideas you may want to pursue in another paragraph.

It can be helpful to set writing time goals for yourself—for instance, you could decide that each time you sit down, you will write for one hour straight without interruptions of any kind. You will be amazed at how much you write if you do a little of this each day. The key is to keep writing.

Writers should reflect on what they have written at the end of each writing session. This is often done away from the computer and even while working on something else. Ideas require time to develop, process, and refine, and many people find that their best ideas often come at random moments. Give yourself space from your actual writing after you have met your writing goal for the day.

Syda Productions/Shutterstock.com

It is always advisable to "sleep on it" after writing your first draft in order to revisit it the next day with "fresh eyes."

The length of the break is ultimately up to you, but one night is a good rule of thumb—it allows enough space from your writing and yet not so much that you lose your momentum. This age-old wisdom is good advice for a first draft of your paper, too. If you complete your first draft in the evening, go to sleep, and then look at it the next day, you may discover that sections causing you difficulty the day before fall more easily into place when you are rested. If you complete a section of your paper or a complete draft in the morning, perhaps you will feel refreshed enough to look at what you have written in the evening: Only you will know when you are ready. Whatever the length of your break, make sure you give yourself a specific time to begin work again—and define the time you will return to your writing before you step away from your draft—so that you do not delay your progress on the assignment. Try to avoid waiting more than two days to return to your writing because that would likely interrupt the development of your ideas—you can get too far away from your writing. Make sure that you write down a tentative thesis statement as part of the first draft process; you will return to this thesis and revise it after allowing yourself some time to process what you have written. When you return to the draft, you will be looking at it with "fresh eyes," and you will probably find that revising is much easier than it would have been if you tried to revise the draft immediately. Begin by rereading what you wrote the day before and making adjustments/ revisions as necessary. Then pick up where you left off at the end of the draft, keeping in mind the day's writing goal.

Planning for Revision and the Thesis Statement

After writing your first draft and taking a break, it is time to concentrate on the next step in the writing process: revising your draft. It is sometimes difficult to know when to stop writing and begin revising. Try to write until you have developed your ideas as fully as possible. Often, it is the case that in writing a draft, ideas that you may think are not your main point could become the focus of a new paragraph. Because ideas and critical thinking emerge while you are writing, a first draft should explore your connections as thoroughly as possible.

When you return to your draft later, reread the paper and ask yourself what main points you are arriving at. Keep in mind that you want to sort out which points best respond to the writing prompt. You may want to write down a tentative introduction and thesis statement and then draft your body paragraphs, but keep in mind that if you do this, your thesis statement is not a permanent contract. The trouble with writing a thesis statement first is that you are guessing what you are going to argue in your body paragraphs before you have written them. What you end up arguing needs to then be reflected in your thesis. Return to your thesis statement multiple times and revise it to make sure it reflects what you argue in your body paragraphs and that it directly responds to the writing prompt. A more natural way to arrive at your thesis statement is to write your body paragraphs first in an effort to discover your argument and develop your ideas. You would then reread your paragraphs several times and try to determine what main point you are working toward. Then go back and write your introductory paragraph and thesis. No matter which method you decide to use, all writing should be revised and refined until you have put forward your best, most specific, response to the writing prompt. You never should feel that what you have written on the page is something you cannot change.

8.2 Revising

Revision is the process of rereading, reflecting upon, and improving drafts or drafting materials. Revising often leads to rewriting, more revision, and more rewriting, as Figure 8.1 illustrates. This cycle may be repeated several times before you have a final version of your paper. Sometimes you must revise a great deal, and sometimes you must revise only a little until you meet all the criteria listed earlier in this chapter.

Figure 8.1: The revising process

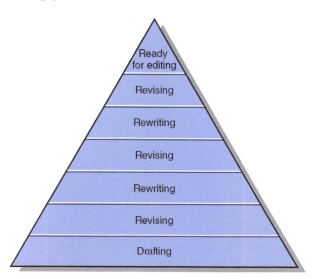

Revising With Feedback

While it is very important that you spend time carefully revising and improving your paper, it can be just as useful to obtain feedback from your peers or from your instructor. Your instructor might comment on portions of working drafts, or create peer editing groups, or groups of your classmates who will review and comment on your draft essay. You might be given peer editing instructions or a commenting sheet to direct the peer editing feedback. Whatever method your class uses for commenting on drafts, make sure that you ask for clarification if you have any questions about what the feedback means. Allow plenty of time in between peer editing or instructor feedback and your next phase of revision and development. Requests to instructors that occur the day before the paper is due are generally too late to sufficiently incorporate feedback. Check with your instructor about the class policy on this.

WAYHOME studio/Shutterstock.com

Revising is the process of viewing your paper as a whole to ensure that it is focused, well organized, coherent, and complete.

Revising Specific Components of the Essay

Revising does not mean just reading over your paper to make sure it does not contain any errors. It means focusing your brain on the paper as a whole, not on individual words. It requires taking a big-picture view of the paper and looking at it from a holistic, visual, and organizational point of view. You might consider putting yourself in the shoes of your readers when you revise and trying to determine whether what you have written will be clear and understandable to your audience. You have four primary goals when you revise: to make sure your paper is

- Focused
- Well structured and well organized
- Complete
- Coherent.

The purpose of revising is to make sure you have covered everything necessary in your paper, to make sure that you have directly responded to the writing prompt, to make sure that you have included sufficient evidence to support your main ideas, to make sure that you have sufficiently analyzed this evidence, and to improve your organization of ideas. When you revise, you will probably reorganize ideas, move information around so that ideas flow better, combine and restructure information into well-constructed paragraphs, rewrite content, and add material to support your ideas. You will also likely delete a lot of what you have written. It is ideal that when you write your first draft you write much more length-wise than what the assignment is asking for. Then you can go back and locate the best ideas and develop those more fully, while deleting the content that is off track or that does not directly respond to the prompt. When you revise, ask yourself the following four questions.

Is the Paper Focused?

Does your paper have a single focus and a clear thesis statement, and does other material in the paper relate to and support this thesis? Each body paragraph should directly support your thesis statement, and every body paragraph should also offer evidence to support your main point. This can mean quoting from a text or referring to specific details from a personal experience, if you are writing a personal essay. Ask yourself whether everything you have written in the paper is relevant. **Relevance** deals with how well the content of your paper relates to your thesis and to the assignment. Every paragraph in your paper should have a reason or serve a purpose; if it does not, it should be removed. A great way to test this is to read your entire paper out loud to yourself. It is generally much easier to hear places in your writing that are unclear than if you just read the paper silently.

Is the Paper Well Structured and Well Organized?

Make sure your paper has a clear introduction, body, and conclusion and that each section includes all the required elements discussed in the writing prompt. Verify that the main points in the body of your paper are clear and organized into effective paragraphs. Look at your paper visually. Are your ideas divided into standard paragraphs? What exactly is a standard paragraph? A paragraph should generally not be longer than a page or page and a half at most. Your paragraphs do not all have to be the same length, but bear in mind that overly short paragraphs that are only a few sentences are certainly not sufficiently developed. For most essays, a paragraph should not be shorter than about half a page. In some cases with personal essays or in writing a creative short story, it may be appropriate to occasionally write a very brief paragraph.

Every paragraph should include at least a topic sentence that directly relates to the thesis, specific evidence to support it, and several sentences of analysis explaining how that evidence supports your paragraph's main claim. It can be helpful to step back and look at your paper visually. Make sure that your paragraphs are not significantly longer than a page each. If you find one that is, it is likely that you have a subpoint in your paragraph, and should create new paragraph when that subpoint begins. You should always ask your instructor if you are uncertain what the assignment is asking you to do.

Is the Paper Complete?

Does your paper meet the assignment length? Often writing instructors do not mind if you write a page beyond the requirement, but not writing enough is usually a problem because it means that you have not developed a complete enough response to the prompt. Review your paper to make sure you have included all the information necessary. Did you develop a main point that directly responds to the prompt and develops that idea over the course of several paragraphs? Go back and read the assignment to make sure you met all requirements. If you have overlooked something, add the missing material to your paper.

Writers often do not understand how to include enough evidence into the body paragraphs. Ideas cannot stand alone—writers always have to make sure to provide specific evidence in every body paragraph; otherwise the ideas are unsupported. There is no perfect number of quotes that should occur in each paragraph, but each should have either direct citation or paraphrase (though paraphrasing tends to have the best use in research papers when one is paraphrasing historical information). To analyze a text carefully, one must directly cite it. Only add additional quotes to a paragraph if they add something new to the discussion.

Part of the purpose in a paper is to prove how your interpretation is supportable by concrete evidence and to explain how that evidence supports the ideas. In almost all cases, a writing assignment asks writers to prove on the page how the interpretation is a reasonable, well-supported one. Even if an instructor asks for a personal essay in which you are to explain how you arrived at a position to a controversial topic, then you will still need to use ample evidence to support your ideas.

Is the Paper Coherent?

The word *coherent* means "sticking together," and revising for **coherence** means reviewing your work to determine whether the connections between your ideas are clear and whether your writing flows well. Writing that is coherent is easy to read and understand. Again, reading out loud is an excellent method to check for coherence. It is much easier to hear problems with coherence and moments when your writing may have gotten off track than it is to catch these problems by simply reading the paper silently to yourself. If your paper is coherent, it will not seem "choppy," and readers will be able to follow along with your ideas as they read. Coherence is achieved by organizing ideas well, and part of this means including transitions appropriately.

Coherence also means organizing your ideas in a way that is logical, so that your ideas and paragraphs progress, one building block at a time. The specific organization of your paper depends entirely on the writing assignment. You might organize your ideas so that they follow the progress of a novel, poem, or drama chronologically, or you might organize your ideas so that they develop thematically. For certain assignments, you might set up causes first and later discuss the effects of a particular study or problem.

If you have progressed to this step in the writing process and find you are having trouble, do not forget that help is available to you from several sources. If you have followed the steps above and still need assistance understanding the assignment or generating ideas, contact your instructor or teaching assistant to see whether they can offer any guidance.

8.3 Editing

There is revising your paper for content, and then there is **editing** your paper for clarity of language. Both processes are completely essential to writing a good paper. You should not worry much about editing your sentences for grammar and clarity while you are developing your ideas. It is simply trying to accomplish too many things at the same time to develop your ideas and write them flawlessly on the page all at once—and it is unrealistic. No writer can do this in the first draft of a paper. Remember that revising is a big-picture view, whereas editing considers individual elements and details very closely. When you edit, you scrutinize issues such as language choices, the clarity and conciseness of your writing, spelling, grammar, punctuation, and sentence structure. You edit when you believe the content of your paper is complete or mostly complete. However, if new ideas develop that help you to respond more fully to the writing prompt, by all means, add them to the paper.

You might want to take a short break between revising and editing to "switch gears" for the analysis you must perform during the editing step. It is impossible to look at all editing issues at once, so you must make several passes through your paper to read what you have written, word for word. A good practice is to check one of the editing issues discussed below in each of your editing passes.

Style and Language

When you write, your language focuses readers' attention and creates impressions in their minds. The language you choose depends on three factors: the purpose of the writing, the audience, and the genre. Your college papers have an academic audience and will be read by your instructors and teaching assistants, and perhaps by some of your peers in your class. Recall that genre refers to a category of writing that has a particular form and technique. Appropriate language and tone for one genre is not always appropriate for another. Fiction writing, poetry, journalistic writing, business writing, marketing communications, and technical writing are all different genres. Academic writing, for example, is a specific genre that tends to use a formal, educated, academic voice. In this text, for example, we have adopted a conversational tone, as we would in a classroom discussion. However, as we discussed earlier, college papers require formal language. In your college writing assignments, you should avoid slang, jargon, and contractions. Avoid informal language that you would use with friends and avoid using sayings or clichés. Often informal types of language such as these are a replacement for what a writer should be saying in a paper—what she is arguing, how it is supported, and what the evidence suggests. The personal essay is at times an exception to this rule, particularly if you are asked to write about a personal experience.

Tone and Voice

Language also creates what is known as the tone of your writing. The tone of a piece of writing may be positive, negative, warm, friendly, serious, sincere, humorous, or hostile, to name a few possibilities. Most college writing assignments are formal essays that require you to write in a way that follows the conventions of formal writing—a clear, serious, academic tone that seeks to treat the reader of the essay as an educated audience. This means that your tone should always convey respect for your audience.

Remember that when you write a college paper that is a persuasive essay, and your purpose is to convince readers to take some action, you might occasionally make an emotional appeal to your readers. However, you must persuade primarily with logic and factual evidence, not simply by appealing to emotions. Educated readers immediately know when someone is trying to persuade them simply through emotions, and you would never want your readers to feel manipulated—instead, you want them to think that you have argued persuasively and effectively through sound reasoning, logic, and evidence. So, in these papers as well, edit to avoid language that is overly emotional and attempt to find more neutral terms for emotional words.

Denotations and Connotations

All forms of college writing, besides the personal essay, require language that is not overly emotional. But what does *overly emotional* mean? In English, words have two types of meaning: denotations and connotations. The **denotation**, or denotative meaning, is the most descriptive and neutral dictionary definition of a word. The **connotation** is what the word suggests or implies. Connotations give words their emotional impact, and this impact can be either positive or negative. For example, the description of a person as "careful with money," uses fairly neutral denotative words to describe that person. However, calling a person "stingy" creates a negative tone because the words has a strong negative connotation. On the other hand, calling someone "thrifty" or "prudent" creates a positive tone and a strong positive connotation of that person in the reader's mind. Remember that the language you choose reflects your attitude toward people, places, and things.

Trigger Words

We know from our conversations with others that people often react strongly to certain language. Some words are **trigger words** that evoke such a strong emotional response in us that we focus on the word itself instead of what we are listening to or reading. We all have our own personal trigger words. However, some words are positive or negative to almost everyone. For example, consider advertisements you have seen. Advertisers are very aware of universal trigger words, so they do not say, "Buy our diet product; it will make you skinny." Instead, they use words with positive connotations and tell you their product will make you *slim* or *slender*. Consider your audience and always avoid offensive or sexist language in your writing.

Synonyms

Most words have **synonyms**, words that have similar meanings but may have very different connotations. When you edit, make sure to keep a thesaurus handy or use the thesaurus in Microsoft Word® and review your writing to make sure your language is appropriate for the academic writing genre. The tone of your college writing should be clear and objective and should use words with neutral, denotative meanings. Academic writing calls for serious, professional, and scholarly writing, which is largely achieved by appropriate language choices and an engaged response to the writing prompt that shows a serious attempt to answer the question.

Clarity and Conciseness

After checking the language in your paper, make a second editing pass to see if your writing is clear and concise. Clear writing is the result of expressing your ideas so that they are understandable, and not confusing, to readers. You achieve clarity by making good language choices such as using neutral, denotative words; avoiding slang and jargon; being specific and not vague in your descriptions; and writing with a serious and professional tone. You also must make your essay as grammatically correct as possible because grammatical errors can profoundly impact the clarity of your writing—your ideas may be very good, but if they are not clear because what you are saying is not understandable, your readers will have no idea what your good ideas are. If grammatical errors are a significant concern for you, plan to get help early and often to work on these errors.

When writing is concise, it contains no unnecessary words. Conciseness is achieved by making good language choices, focusing on subjects and verbs in your sentences, and eliminating repetition and redundancies. Do not use multiple adjectives to describe one item in a sentence—instead, choose the one adjective that is the most adequate descriptor. Likewise, avoid using multiple verbs as synonyms side by side in a sentence. Of particular concern is to avoid using passive voice, which includes versions of the verb "to be." You can use the word "is," however, to describe something: "She is highly intelligent."

8.4 Proofreading

Proofreading is not editing; when you proofread, your job is not to look for possible language changes or to check whether punctuation and grammar is correct. These tasks should have been completed during editing, but if you do happen to find more edits you should make, you should of course go ahead and complete these. Try to make sure you complete each step as thoroughly as you can before you move on to the next one because it is much easier to focus on only one or two elements at a time. The purpose of proofreading is to take one last look at your paper to see if what is actually on the page is what you think you wrote. To accomplish this task, you must shift your focus from reading sentences to reading individual words, and you must read everything on the page such as page headers, page numbers, symbols, numbers, bullets, and punctuation marks.

Elena Elisseeva/Shutterstock.com

After all edits have been performed, you should always go back through your paper looking for errors in spelling, punctuation, and formatting.

Proofreading Strategies

If you have been working on the computer screen while you revised and edited, print your paper and proofread from the printed copy, with a pencil in hand so that you can mark errors as you find them. It is generally more effective to proofread from a printed page than to do so on the computer screen because you can see the errors more easily. Taking a break between editing and proofreading is also recommended. Proofreading is usually improved if you can look at your paper with fresh eyes.

When we read a paper we have written, we are often so absorbed in our subject that we see what we think we wrote, not what is actually there. So, to proofread effectively, we must fool our brain so that we read only one word at a time or one line of text at a time, not sentences and paragraphs, as we do with normal reading. Many people, therefore, adopt special proofreading strategies to make sure they accomplish that goal. Below are some strategies for you to try. Experiment with different methods until you find one that works well for you or try a combination of strategies.

- *Read aloud to yourself.* Reading your paper aloud helps you determine the flow, or coherence, of your writing. It can enable you to recognize sentences that are awkward or difficult to understand. It can also help you identify sentences that are too long. If you run out of breath before you get to the period at the end of the sentence, you know that the sentence needs to be shorter. If you try to read through a sentence and you simply cannot or you stumble as you read, it is a sure sign that the sentence needs to be revised for clarity and/or for grammatical errors. Remember, when you proof-read, read only one word at a time and read all punctuation marks aloud as well.

- *Read aloud to someone else.* Many writers belong to writing groups, and one of the benefits of such groups is that you can obtain feedback from others. Reading a paper aloud to someone else can help both you and your listener assess the coherence of the paper. Additionally, it enables others to give you input as to whether your ideas are clear and understandable. Peer editors are a very useful part of the revision process. An instructor may set up peer editing groups, or you may talk with someone in your class and ask to work as peer editors for one another. A different perspective offers insight into the areas that can be strengthened.

- *Read aloud while someone else reads along silently.* Print two copies of your paper and proofread with another person. Read your paper aloud to someone else while he or she reads along silently; if you wish, you can switch roles halfway through. The person reading aloud is more likely to find problems with sentence length, coherence, and clarity while the person reading silently will often more easily see punctuation errors. You could exchange papers with someone else in your class and promise to give each other extensive feedback. Peer editing is a very valuable technique for strengthening your papers.

- *Have someone else proofread for you.* If you are fortunate to have someone else who can proofread your paper for you, you might want to take advantage of the oppor-tunity. Someone who is not as close to the paper as you are might be able to spot errors you might overlook. Remember, though, the accuracy of the final paper is your responsibility. Your instructors are not proofreaders, but there may be resources at your school that can assist you with some proofreading.

- *Proofread in a different location.* Sometimes, moving away from the computer and reading your paper while you are curled up on the sofa or sitting at the kitchen table will give you a different perspective and enable you to find errors more easily.

- *Proofread with an index card.* You might try moving an index card or a piece of paper along as you proofread and covering words to the right of the word you are reading. This technique forces you to read only one word at a time and to read more carefully and slowly than you otherwise would.

- *Proofread with a ruler.* Another technique is to place a ruler under each line of text as you read. Move the rule down the page, line by line, while you are reading. This proofreading strategy forces you to read the line of text, not the sentence, and can assist you in finding unnecessary words and sentence structure errors.

Microsoft Word® Tools

After you have edited the language in your paper, read through your paper again and edit for proper spelling, grammar, punctuation, and sentence structure. You can obtain help for this task from the automatic spelling- and grammar-checking features in Microsoft Word®. Remember, however, that suggestions made by automatic checkers are not always correct, so do not depend on them completely. Instead, check your paper yourself first; then use the automatic checking features on the word processing software to check yourself and see whether you missed anything.

References and Formatting

Make sure to review the format of your paper to ensure that it conforms to the required documentation style. Make sure your margins are correct, that your paper is appropriately spaced and paragraphs are indented as required, that your page header is included and properly formatted, and that your title page and reference page (if needed) are prepared properly. Also ensure that you have correctly cited all outside sources in the text of your paper and in the reference list.

8.5 The Final Draft

With the final draft in hand, it is useful to take a moment to consider what you have learned and what you can continue to improve on. Writing out some answers to final draft reflective questions can make your future writing goals more concrete. See *Writing in Action: Final Draft Reflection Exercise* for some examples of reflective questions you can ask about your own paper.

Writing in Action: Final Draft Reflection Exercise

Try answering the following questions on a sheet of paper. Stating your outcomes from the writing process helps clarify what you want as a writer and how you will attempt to accomplish those goals in future writing assignments.

1. What are the strongest parts of the essay? Why?
2. Which parts of the essay did you work on the most?
3. If you had more time, what would you continue to work on?
4. What do you think is the weakest part of your paper?
5. For the next paper, what do you hope to improve on?

Finally, congratulate yourself. You have completed all the steps in the writing process, and you should be ready to submit your paper, with the confidence that you have done the best job you can do. Is the paper finished? Author and journalism professor Donald M. Murray writes,

A piece of writing is never finished. It is delivered to a deadline, torn out of the typewriter on demand, sent off with a sense of accomplishment and shame and pride and frustration. If only there were a couple more days, time for just another run at it, perhaps then . . . . (Murray, 2002, p. 58)

A piece of writing is never perfect. Every time you read it, you will probably find something you could change. However, there comes a time when all writers have to give up their desire for perfection and make sure they submit their writing on time. You always want to make sure that you have gone through every step of the drafting process, and in order to do that, you need to avoid procrastination, which is the number one roadblock to writing effective essays. Writing is not like memorizing a set of formulas that you can simply "plug in" to get the "correct" answer—instead, writing is a process of developing your thoughts and articulating a clear position. This takes time to do, but it is extremely rewarding because you learn how to articulate yourself better and because it gives an occasion to clarify your thoughts about a subject.

Chapter Summary

No famous writers simply write a masterpiece the very first time they write—all writing is in some sense a draft waiting for improvement. Revising, editing, and proofreading are the cornerstones of all good writing. Writers should never feel pressure to create a perfect work of art during the initial drafting stage. This unrealistic ideal only hinders the writing process and adds unnecessary pressure. Sentences are not lifelong contracts; they are always tentative, waiting for the benefit of another reading and revision. Because it is impossible to create an ideal paper in one sitting, writing calls for planning and organizing one's time carefully. Yet writing has many rewards—there is not only the obvious reward of performing well on a paper, but there is also the less tangible reward of learning from the writing process. Writing creates more capable thinkers by promoting analytical thought and inquiry into important subjects.

Key Terms

coherence Clear connections between ideas that facilitate the logical flow of a paper.

connotation What a word suggests or implies. Connotations give words their emotional impact, and this impact can be either positive or negative.

denotation The most descriptive and neutral dictionary definition of a word.

editing A close check of the individual elements and details in a paper. Editing focuses on issues such as language choices, the clarity and conciseness of the writing, spelling, grammar, punctuation, and sentence structure.

proofreading A final review of a paper to ensure that what the author intended to write is what the paper actually conveys. Proofreading includes reading individual words and reading everything on the page such as page headers, page numbers, symbols, numbers, bullets, and punctuation marks.

relevance How well the content of a paper relates to the paper's thesis and to the assignment.

revision The process of rereading, reflecting upon, and improving drafts or drafting materials; includes attending to the responsiveness to the writing prompt, organization, cohesion, the thesis, argument development, use of evidence, grammar, spelling, and proper formatting.

synonyms Words that have similar meanings but that may have very different connotations.

trigger words Words that evoke such a strong emotional response in the reader that he or she tends to focus on the word itself instead of what is being read or listened to.

Revision...Or Something Else

9

WAYHOME studio/Shutterstock.com

We often think about revising as something we do *after* we have written a paper, and the worksheets at the back of this textbook along with the Revision Ideas at the end of each section can help you realize your ideas by giving you ways to restructure, reorganize, and develop them. Rewriting what you have written often improves what you have committed to words. Typically, however, when you approach revision wholeheartedly, your work may look a little worse before it looks better. If you consider everything you have written worthy of a second look, and based on a reappraisal of your words you decide to add to the writing or change it somehow, the changing does not occur without new problems arising. This is all right. Though it may feel challenging to see your work lose its solidity as you reconsider it, you might think of the process as one in which you are searching for a truth. While writing a paper for a college course carries with it some responsibility and—one would hope—some payoff, you may be after something more important than a grade or even a degree. You may want for yourself an ability to recognize your own insights, to build on them, to manage them so that others can benefit from them, and to know that because you thought hard about what you wanted to say exactly, you grew, and others came to appreciate the way you think. This is no slight contribution you are making. Separate yourself from the preponderance of expectations put upon you to perform well in college and you may just discover a great number of things you never expected. Your journey in college depends on your ability to articulate your experience. This is true also for your relationships, for your future career, and for the best parts of your life.

All writers and student writers who have something insightful to say have revised their writing. Almost without exception, all writers dread revising their writing. It is hard work. But it is hard in the way you realize that loving someone is hard: it is hard sometimes because you care. Most everyone has written a paper last minute and submitted it, hoping for the best. Give yourself the credit and the respect you deserve by avoiding that circumstance. Your writing represents you to others who probably do not know you well and have no familiarity with the unique way your mind works. Read your own writing as you would anything you care about because you care about how you make your offering.

You will find in this book after the essay assignment in each chapter several revision ideas to help you get a footing on rereading your own work and finding a way to converse with it. This is an important step in your development. At the ancient Temple of Apollo at Delphi a saying had been written in Greek that read, "Know Thyself." It is the first thought given to worshippers before entering the temple. It should be fair enough to continue the tradition today of making our primary charge looking inward before we give our gifts to the world. Joining the conversations other essayists have had in these pages should guide your entrance into conversations with your own writing, which has to be the primary source of your understanding. In other words, your understanding of what you read, see, hear, and experience comes first and foremost from your understanding of yourself and who you are. Everything you do for this course should help you understand yourself, and everything else you do should be predicated on knowing yourself well.

9.1 Methods for Revising

Below are several methods for revising after you have written something. Use these methods any time but especially if you feel stuck or that you have not said enough. Begin your process of revision as you look at these methods. Reconsider your expectations, your reasons for taking this course, what you want for yourself, even your greater sense of purpose. Anytime someone or something poses a question to you, reframe it to yourself with this idea in mind.

Method 1: Reverse Outlining

Besides reading what others write, you should read your own writing with careful attention and interest. As you write and think about what you want to say, you cannot possibly account for every idea you will have or all the connections you can make. These connections and ideas come with time and deepen with each meaningful visit you pay to your writing.

Reverse outlining shows you what your organization looks like *so far.*

Method 2: Reading Imperatively

By reading the draft of your paper slowly and inquisitively, you can explore the implications and ramifications of what you have already said in order (1) to begin to understand the complexity of your subject, (2) to discover new forces in your paper, and (3) to help clarify your main point or thesis.

Annotate your own paper to explore the implications of what you have written so far. If you need more room for your questions, use extra sheets of paper. Be hyper-inquisitive. Ask a question of anything that moves. Do not wait until the end of a sentence to ask a question, but rather see if you can explain and justify every important word you use. Begin with just your first paragraph. Reading, questioning, and annotating will probably take you about fifteen minutes.

Example:

Consider the sentence below. Read aggressively until you feel you have exhausted the implications of the writing—for now:

> It is conceivable that a unilateral offering of forgiveness might not be received graciously and that the other party may in fact withhold forgiveness until, in its eyes, you have accepted blame.

If you begin at the beginning, you might come up with questions like these:

- "conceivable" To whom? Why use this word and not "probable," "likely," "reasonable"?
- "unilateral" What really makes a unilateral offering unilateral? Intent? Action? Behavior? Attitude? Posturing?
- "forgiveness" Does forgiveness always feel the same? Always a letting go? Are there kinds of forgiveness? Degrees of forgiveness?
- "graciously" Do we have to be treated "graciously" to make peace?
- "party" How did this word come to mean not just a person or group of persons (in the legal manner) but also an event where people have fun together?
- "withhold" Withhold how? Again, by intent, action, behavior, etc.?
- "in its eyes" It seems we are talking about the perception someone else has of us, or our actions, or our intent. Is this statement addressing the fact that we may have little control over how others feel about us?
- "accepted blame" Sounds somewhat clinical. Is it equivalent to the phrase "admitted you are wrong"?

Admittedly, this is somewhat exhaustive—and maybe even exhausting—but the point is that if you unpack your own sentences to understand the implications of what you have written, you can certainly write more, do a better job of clarifying yourself, and maybe even figure out a way of organizing your ideas.

Method 3: Writing Letters

Writing letters to your reader (often your instructor) about your writing can help you clarify to yourself what you want to say and whether you have satisfied yourself with what you have written. Consider the letter a chance to say the kinds of things you would not expect someone to write in a paper. For instance, we might rarely if ever have the chance to step back from our writing and discuss it in the papers we write, so a letter can do the work of a preface or even a foreword, but without the formality even of those formats. When we write letters (or e-mails or texts) we expect some kind of reply, sooner rather than later, and simply expecting a response can help us anticipate the shape of a conversation that we ourselves begin.

After you have finished your paper, write a cover letter about your paper to your instructor. In your letter, discuss the following:

1. Your process of reading and writing to complete the assignment.
2. The biggest obstacle you faced in writing your paper.
3. The point you are making in your paper.

Write this as a letter, with a salutation (Dear Professor ---) and sign your name to it. The more detailed your letter, the clearer you will be about how you accomplished the tasks involved in completing the paper assignment. The purpose of the letter, a casual accompaniment to your more formal paper, is to relax and be yourself as you discuss your work. If you cannot remember your writing process easily or can't identify the point in your paper, you must take a conscious inventory of the steps that brought you to the finished paper.

Method 4: Providing Support for Assertions

Consider that each time you make a claim that is not self-evident you must provide supporting statements. Otherwise, a claim would be a mere opinion. Opinions come easily, but thoughtful, supported opinions can have the power to sway someone's thinking. Examine the statements below to see how offering supporting statements for the assertion sometimes adds more assertions that in turn must be supported:

Greed is bad, but it is not always bad. Being greedy means taking more than belongs to you at the moment, and the insinuation is that you have not earned what you take. Our society maintains that taking what does not belong to you rightfully is stealing. However, the desire to

Muk Photo/Shutterstock.com

get more—or to take more—drives creative and ambitious entrepreneurs, and this drive stimulates business and the exchange of goods and services, which in turn stimulates the economy.

Here is the statement broken down into its component assertions and statements of support.

Assertion:

Greed is bad, but it is not always bad.

Support 1:

Being greedy means taking more than belongs to you at the moment, and the insinuation is that you have not earned what you take. (This is a definition, and it seems fairly self-evident.)

Support 2:

Our society maintains that taking what does not belong to you rightfully is stealing. (While this may be true, the first statement of support is made in the context of greed, not outright thievery, so it requires support that explains the assertion implied that greediness is equivalent to stealing.)

Support 3:

However, the desire to get more—or to take more—drives creative and ambitious entrepreneurs, and this drive stimulates business and the exchange of goods and services, which in turn stimulates the economy. (This statement of support sounds reasonable, but it makes multiple assertions as well that in turn need supporting statements to clarify those assertions and to make them appear sound or cogent.)

The writer of this statement has several options, but if each assertion is given three statements of support, the writer will find more material than can be handled in a paragraph. In fact, the writer may want to consider developing the statements of support in paragraphs that follow.

A graphic representation of the assertion and support chain above follows:

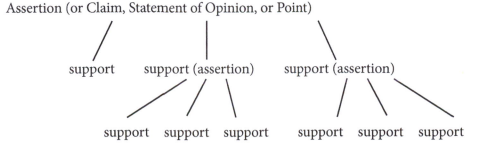

If you feel more comfortable doing math problems than writing papers, you might recall the method by which you learned to find the prime factors of a number. The same idea applies, that of looking for the most basic blocks that build up an idea. For instance:

```
        24
       / \
      8 × 3
     / \
    4 × 2
   / \
  2 × 2
```

If it seems exasperating to bombard yourself with twenty questions every time you write a sentence, rethink your response for a moment. The more questions your writing raises, the more places you can go with your writing, and the more you can explore, understand, and relate. And, frankly, no one asks questions of anything uninteresting. When you run out of questions, you will be tempted to refer to that state as "writer's block," but the fact is "writer's block" only occurs when you stop asking questions.

That Something Else: Reframing

10

The definition of revision as a process of altering something that has already been written falls short of what revision really means in practice. Revision in writing can lead to clarity and a better sense of the purpose of your writing. But real revision, the kind that deserves a more expansive term—*reframing*—begins at the very beginning of your work.

If someone asks us something and we do not quite understand what is being asked, we might ask a question in return. This is the first step in reframing. It naturally occurs in conversation, and it is a form of active or responsive listening. If someone should ask us, "Where were you on December 11 of last year?" we might want to know why they are asking even before we think about, if we have any chance at all of remembering where we were at any given time during that day. Not to ask a question in return puts us in a compromising position. Of course, this is—one would hope—a far-fetched example, but it proves the point. Instead of wondering why we are being asked for this information, we have to know why, not because our answer is predicated on knowing why someone has asked us a particular question but because our *response* is predicated on knowing. The way we process our response to a question depends largely on understanding what the question means to us. Did we forget an anniversary? Were quarterly taxes due on that day? Do the police want to know? Does someone who had a party I had promised to come to, but then forgot altogether about it, want to know?

More importantly, I have to think about how I feel receiving such a question. It puts one on alert, doesn't it? And so often as students we can feel the same way when we encounter a question in class.

When we attempt to see the agenda behind the question, we begin to frame or reframe the question for ourselves. This action puts us squarely in the process of revision, or as it goes, reframing. Once we begin to reframe or revise, we take control of all the automatic processes that occur when we engage in an activity. To revise is to be in charge of our own understanding. It is nothing less than this.

Glossary

abstract words Words that have no physical substance; we cannot see, hear, touch, smell, or taste them.

active reading A series of strategies that help you engage with a text, including highlighting and circling key terms, writing question marks and exclamation points, and writing notes in the margins of the text.

alliteration Repetition of initial consonants in words in a series.

analytical paper A paper in which a writer offers an interpretation of a text, event, circumstance, or other objects of analysis.

annotating Writing a note—in the margin of the document you are reading or on a separate piece of paper—that explains or comments on what you have read.

antithesis The rhetorical strategy of placing two opposing ideas together in a sentence for contrasting effect.

appeals to emotion Attempts to create an emotional response in the audience in order to persuade that audience to do or believe something.

argument The position a writer takes on a subject, or an interpretation he or she makes about a text. An argument is not a statement of fact; it is an interpretation that can be disagreed with.

audience The individuals for whom an author is writing or to whom he or she is speaking.

backing The fourth element of Toulmin's model, which consists of additional support for the warrant.

bibliography A list of books referenced in a text that appears toward the end of the material.

block arrangement A type of organizational arrangement that mentions all the features about one subject before it moves on to another subject.

blog An online journal space in which a writer frequently records thoughts, either publicly or privately, on a particular topic.

body The section of an essay that consists of all of the paragraphs except for the introduction and conclusion. The body of the essay is the place where writers develop the thesis and prove the argument by using evidence.

brainstorming Summarizing your main ideas, questions, and responses to a text you are reading in order to try to find main points. This process can help you organize your thoughts before writing a first draft of a paper.

causal chain A type of analysis that perceives a sequence of events in which one event causes the next.

cause-and-effect paper A type of paper that assess the factors that led to a particular effect.

chronological order A type of organization that presents tasks in the order in which they are performed and information in the order in which it occurred in time, usually from earliest to latest.

claim A statement that asserts an argument about a subject, text, or topic.

classification A method of organizing information by grouping items into categories with other items that share similar characteristics.

clustering A method of brainstorming that involves grouping ideas together and branching them off into separate bubbles that contain different ideas.

code switching Alternating languages and/or style according to what one's audience will understand. Code switching might include the use of informal language, multiple languages, expressions, or acronyms that only certain audiences will understand.

coherence Clear connections between ideas that facilitate the logical flow of a paper.

combination paper An assignment that includes elements of personal, expository, persuasive or argument, and research papers. For instance, one section of the paper might be personal, while another is persuasive.

comparison-and-contrast paper A type of expository paper that assesses the main similarities and differences between two or more subjects.

conclusion The end of your discussion of the topic and the closure to your paper. The conclusion should offer an explanation of what all of the main points *add up to*.

concrete words Words that represent people, places, and things we can see, hear, touch, smell, or taste; they are specific and tangible, and represent physical objects rather than ideas, qualities, or concepts.

connotation What a word suggests or implies. Connotations give words their emotional impact, and this impact can be either positive or negative.

creative tension The stress and interest created when a story has an unresolved problem or disagreement, a decision that must be made, or a dilemma or conflict that must be resolved.

creative writing Written or artistic works whose purpose is to create images or to express thoughts or feelings. These works may also imply a position or argument.

critical thinking The mental process of conceptualizing, applying, analyzing, synthesizing, and evaluating information to arrive at a conclusion.

deductive reasoning A form or reasoning wherein you begin by making a general statement and then apply that generalization to a specific situation.

defining terms Explaining what a term means by labeling it and/or providing synonyms.

denotation The most descriptive and neutral dictionary definition of a word.

description A pattern of writing that involves providing details about the physical characteristics of a person, place, object, or event.

description Characterizing or giving qualities in order to make something vivid to the reader.

descriptive language Words that are vivid, expressive, and highly specific to the topic you are writing on.

dialogue A verbal exchange between two or more characters in a text.

editing A close check of the individual elements and details in a paper. Editing focuses on issues such as language choices, the clarity and conciseness of the writing, spelling, grammar, punctuation, and sentence structure.

ethos A speaker's or writer's credibility or authority to speak on a particular subject.

evidence Consists of personal examples, facts, statistics, or the words of credible outside authorities or other believable sources. Opinions, on the other hand, are not legitimate pieces of evidence.

expository writing A type of writing that shares information or explains a subject to readers.

facts Statements that are not in dispute or that can be proven to be true by reasoning, experiment, or personal experience.

fallacy Faulty logic or a pattern of mistaken reasoning.

formal language The standard and most appropriate language for academic and professional papers, legal documents, and business writing. Formal language usually sounds serious, is grammatically correct, and avoids language that would otherwise be used in more casual settings.

formal outline A type of outline that may contain numbers or letters to order an essay's main points. It usually also includes the evidence or quotes the paper will use for each body paragraph.

free-writing An informal method of writing out ideas to get some thoughts on paper without worrying about issues of grammar, mechanics, and structure.

genre The type of writing being used in a given writing situation.

grounds The second element in the Toulmin model, which consists of the proof or the evidence the writer provides to support his or her claim.

hook The first few sentences of a paper that should capture readers' attention and interest them enough that they want to keep reading.

index A list, usually toward the end of a text, that includes the names of authors, themes, and concepts covered in the text. It is a guide that tells you what the text covers and gives page numbers that correspond to that entry.

inductive reasoning Method of reasoning often used in the sciences, wherein you argue from the specific to the general by observing a specific situation, analyzing it, and making a generalization from the facts you observe.

informal language The type of language used when speaking or writing to acquaintances or friends. It may include slang, incomplete sentences, improper capitalization (or no capitalization at all), incorrect grammar, and contractions.

informative writing A type of expository writing that provides the reader with facts about a particular topic, such as a description of how something works.

introduction The beginning of your discussion of the topic and the rest of the paper. A good introduction accomplishes four primary goals: captures the readers' attention and interests them in reading more; reveals the purpose of the paper and the topic; presents the thesis statement; and previews the main points covered in the body of the paper.

irony A figure of speech that illustrates a contrast between reality and appearance.

jargon A specialized language particular to a group of people, usually of a particular profession or group. Specialized language can exclude those who do not belong to the group because they may not understand the language or terms being used.

logos An attempt to persuade by using reasoning and logic. This may include using clear examples, facts, or statistics.

mechanism description A type of analytical paper in which one breaks a simple or complex piece of equipment into its component parts, describes those parts, and attempts to show how it works.

metaphor An implied comparison between two unlike things (without using "like" or "as").

mind map A visual map of ideas for a paper.

narration Storytelling from the perspective of a narrator. The story may be true, false, imaginary, or a combination.

nonfiction A genre of writing that includes biographies, memoirs, and historical documents.

objective Based on facts, rather than on personal opinion, about a given topic.

occasion The reason for writing, or what someone is writing for.

opinion A personal viewpoint on a subject that may or may not be supported with facts or evidence.

opinion paper A type of essay that explains the writer's point of view or opinion on a specific topic.

outlining A process of arranging ideas into an intended organization for a paper. It usually contains a formal letter and number style, and specific information such as a tentative thesis statement.

pathos An attempt to persuade by making appeals to the audience's emotions.

personal essay A type of essay that typically uses the first person to convey the thoughts, feelings, experiences, and ideas of the writer. It may or may not take a position at some point in the essay. Most of the topic sentences in a personal essay are not argumentative.

personal journal A place to record ongoing personal experiences. Personal journals can be shared broadly or with no one. It is helpful to keep a personal journal to keep track of ideas for a writing assignment.

personal writing A type of writing in which the writer states his or her opinion about an issue; documents his or her observations; relates a subject to his or her own life; shares a story; or provides a description of a person, place, object, or event. Personal opinion, narrative essays, and some types of reflection papers fall into this category.

persona The voice used when writing or speaking; a unique character to one's own writing.

persuasion An attempt to influence others to adopt a certain belief or point of view or to convince them to take some action.

plagiarism The use of another person's or writer's language, research, or ideas without citing and giving credit to that source of information. Any ideas or language that derive from someone else's writing must be cited, even when paraphrasing.

plot The order, or sequence, of events that unfold in a story.

point-by-point arrangement A method of arranging a comparison-and-contrast paper in which one compares or contrasts subjects point by point, choosing one feature at a time and alternating between the subjects when discussing that feature.

position paper An essay in which you take a stand, or state your opinion, on a controversial issue. Your purpose is to convince your readers that your position on the issue is the best or the correct one.

post hoc ergo propter hoc A Latin phrase meaning "after this therefore because of this."

premises Foundational claims that form the basis of the argument and that lead to a logical conclusion.

problem–solution paper A type of analytical paper in which the author defines a problem, suggests alternative solutions to the problem, and discusses each potential solution.

proofreading A final review of a paper to ensure that what the author intended to write is what the paper actually conveys. Proofreading includes reading individual words and reading everything on the page such as page headers, page numbers, symbols, numbers, bullets, and punctuation marks.

proposals Persuasive reports that identify a problem and recommend a solution to that problem.

qualifier The fifth element of Toulmin's model, which consists of the degree of force or probability to be attached to the claim.

reading journal A space where readers organize thoughts and questions about a text. It may include definitions of words that needed to be looked up, reflections on the text, or questions about moments in the text that are not clearly resolved or that seem perplexing.

reflective paper An assignment that asks the writer think about something he or she has read and to respond to it or discuss its meaning for him or her.

relevance How well the content of a paper relates to the paper's thesis and to the assignment.

research writing A type of writing that requires the writer to discuss a subject using information gathered from outside sources. These types of assignments may also be called *term papers*, *informative* or *analytical reports*, or *case studies*.

reservation The final element in the Toulmin model, which consists of the statements the writer makes that acknowledge exceptions or limitations to the argument or conditions under which the argument would not apply.

response paper An assignment that requires the writer to think about the different points of view expressed in the material being discussed and to take a personal stand on the issue.

reverse outline A type of outline that is written after an essay has been drafted.

revision The process of rereading, reflecting upon, and improving drafts or drafting materials; includes attending to the responsiveness to the writing prompt, organization, cohesion, the thesis, argument development, use of evidence, grammar, spelling, and proper formatting.

rhetorical devices The use of language, style, or even visual techniques intended to produce a particular effect on the audience.

rhetorical question A question for which an answer is not expected because it is assumed to be obvious.

rhetoric The use of language in order to persuade an audience. Someone who is trying to be persuasive should carefully consider what will be persuasive for the particular audience while writing.

scratch outline A list of ideas that will be covered in an essay. A scratch outline is usually written prior to a formal outline, but in some cases a writer may feel ready to skip the scratch outline.

simile A comparison between two things using the words "like" or "as."

SQ3R method A useful strategy for reading books and other lengthy reading materials. SQ3R is an abbreviation for Survey, Question, Read, Recite, and Review.

statistics Data that can be represented numerically.

style guide A reference book that provides information on how to improve writing, grammar, and punctuation. It also contains essential information and standards that must be followed when writing, such as how to format a paper and how to document any outside sources used.

subject The general area of interest from which the topic of a paper is selected.

subjective Based on one's own observation, experience, or opinion.

synonyms Words that have similar meanings but that may have very different connotations.

thesis statement A sentence that makes an arguable claim that the paper will support and develop over the course of the paper.

tone The mood the writer conveys about the subject matter. The tone could be skeptical, humorous, serious, or sarcastic, for example.

topic A specific area of focus taken from a broader subject.

topic sentences Types of sentences that are typically placed at the beginning of each paragraph and indicate what the writer will argue or try to prove in that one paragraph.

transitions Words, phrases, or sentences that let readers know that you are moving from one idea to another or from one section of the paper to another. Also called *connectives*.

trigger words Words that evoke such a strong emotional response in the reader that her or she tends to focus on the word itself instead of what is being read or listened to.

voice The character of the writer or speaker that is conveyed through the material. A writer's voice is synonymous with persona.

warrants Explanations of how the evidence cited in a paper supports the paper's claims; in essence, it analyzes the evidence and interprets it.

writing situation The occasion, audience, writer's voice, and argument of the writing. The writing situation also determines the genre required.

References

Anzaldúa, G. (1987/2007). How to tame a wild tongue. In S. Cohen (Ed.), *50 essays: A portable anthology* (2nd ed.). Boston, MA: Bedford Books.

Aristotle. (350 BCE). *Rhetoric* (trans. W. Rhys Roberts). Retrieved from http://classics.mit.edu/Aristotle/rhetoric.html

Campsall, D. (2010). Writing that persuades. Retrieved from http://www.englishbiz.co.uk/mainguides/persuade.htm

Carnegie, D. (2009, November 3). *How to make friends and influence people* (Reissue ed.). New York, NY: Simon & Schuster.

Daggett, W. R. (2002). *Jobs and the skills gap* (White paper). Rexford, NY: International Center for Leadership in Education. Retrieved October 16, 2009, from http://www.leadered.com/pdf/Job-Skills%20Gap%20White%20PaperPDF.pdf

Dietz, W. H. (2009, December 16). CDC congressional testimony: Innovative childhood obesity practices. Centers for Disease Control and Prevention, U.S. Department of Health and Human Services. Retrieved from http://www.cdc.gov/washington/testimony/2009/t20091216.htm

Emerson, R. W. (1849/1996). Nature. In J. Porte, H. Bloom, & P. Kane (Eds.), *Ralph Waldo Emerson: Essays and Poems*. First Library of America College Edition. New York: Penguin Books.

Faulkner, W. (1968). *Lion in the garden: Interviews with William Faulkner, 1926–1962*. New York, NY: Random House.

FIFA. (n.d.). Retrieved from http://www.fifa.com

Goldberg, N. (2005). *Writing down the bones: Freeing the writing within*. Boston, MA: Shambhala Publications, Inc.

Halawi, L. A., Pires, S., & McCarthy, R. V. (2009, July/August). An evaluation of e-learning on the basis of Bloom's Taxonomy: An exploratory study. *Journal of Education for Business, 84*(6), 374–381.

Hemingway, E. (1952). *The old man and the sea*. New York, NY: Scribner.

Hoyt, J. K., & Roberts, K. L. (2009). *Hoyt's new encyclopedia of practical quotations*. New York: Bartleby.com. Retrieved February 15, 2010, from http://www1.bartleby.com/78/121.html

Hryciuk, D. (1995, September 12). Literacy sold on site; wise bosses help workers increase their knowledge potential; in Alberta's workplaces; literacy facts; the workplace [Final Edition]. *Edmonton Journal*, p. D7.

Huber, J. A. (2004, Summer). A closer look at SQ3R. *Reading Improvement, 41*(2), 108–112.

Jeffers, S. (2006). *Feel the fear . . . and do it anyway*. New York, NY: Ballantine Books.

Jolliff, W. (1998, May). Text as topos: Using the Toulmin model of argumentation in introduction to literature. *Teaching English in the Two Year College, 25*(2), 151–158.

Lucas, S. E. (1998). *The art of public speaking* (6th ed.). Boston, MA: McGraw-Hill.

Mason, M. (1996). "Introduction." Charlotte Brontë's *Jane Eyre*. New York, NY: Penguin Group.

McBride, J. (1996/2008). "Schul/School." *The color of water*. R. Diyanni (Ed.), *One hundred great essays*. (3rd ed.). New York, NY: Pearson Education.

Millman, D. (1984). *Way of the peaceful warrior: A book that changes lives*. Tiburon, CA: Kramer.

Murray, D. M. (2002). The maker's eye: Revising your own manuscripts. In G. H. Muller (Ed.), *The McGraw Hill reader: Issues across the disciplines* (pp. 56–60). New York: McGraw-Hill.

Newkirk, T., & Miller, L. C. (2009). *The essential Don Murray: Lessons from America's greatest writing teacher*. Portsmouth, NH: Boynton/Cook.

Nordquist, R. (2009). Writers on writing: Overcoming writer's block. *About.com Guide: Grammar and composition*. Retrieved December 20, 2009, from http://grammar.about.com/od/yourwriting/a/wblockquotes.htm

Oates, J. C. (1966). Where are you going, where have you been? As published in Oates, J. C. (1970). *The wheel of love and other stories*. New York, NY: Fawcett Crest Books.

Quindlen, A. (2007). Good boy, Beau. Stay. *Newsweek*. Retrieved from http://www.thedailybeast.com/newsweek/2007/04/15/good-boy-beau-stay.html

Rapp, C. (2010). Aristotle's rhetoric. *Stanford Encyclopedia of Philosophy*. Stanford, CA: Metaphysics Research Lab, Center for the Study of Language and Information, Stanford University. Retrieved from http://plato.stanford.edu/entries/aristotle-rhetoric/

Rovell, D. (2008, February 12). CNBC special report: Swoosh! Inside Nike. Michael Jordan continues to score points for footwear giant. MSNBC. Retrieved from http://www.msnbc.msn.com/id/23071595/ns/business-cnbc_tv/page/2/

Ruddell, M. P. 1997. *Teaching content reading and writing* (2nd ed.). Boston: Allyn & Bacon.

San Antonio Light. (1977, May 18). What they're saying, pp. 7-B, 28.

Smith, J. M. (1992). "'Cooped Up': Feminine Domesticity in *Frankenstein*." Mary Shelley's *Frankenstein*. Boston, MA: Bedford Books.

Sophocles. (1984). Antigone. In *The three Theban plays: Antigone, Oedipus the King, Oedipus at Colonus* (trans. Robert Fagles). Penguin Classics. New York, NY: Penguin Books. (Original work published 442 BCE)

Strunk, W., Jr., & White, E. B. (1959). *The elements of style.* New York: Macmillan.

Tan, A. (1990/2007). Mother tongue. In *50 essays: A portable anthology* (2nd ed.). Boston, MA: Bedford Books.

ThinkExist. (2006, January). Linus Pauling quotation. Retrieved from http://en.thinkexist.com/quotes/Dr._Linus_Pauling/

ThinkExist. (2010). Joseph Addison quotation. Retrieved March 28, 2010, from http://thinkexist.com/quotations/reading/3.html

Twain, M. (1868/2007). SLC to Emeline B. Beach, 10 Feb 1868, Washington, D.C. (UCCL 00192). In H. E. Smith, R. Bucci, & L. Salamo (Eds.), *Mark Twain's Letters, 1867–1868.* Mark Twain Project Online. Berkeley, Los Angeles, London: University of California Press. Retrieved from http://www.marktwainproject.org/xtf/view?docId=letters/UCCL00192.xml;style=let ter;brand=mtp

Twain, M. (1895). *The adventures of Huckleberry Finn.* New York, NY: Charles L. Webster and Company. Retrieved from http://www.gutenberg.org/files/76/old/orig76-h/main.htm

U.S. Department of Health and Human Services, Office of the Surgeon General. (2010, January 28). *The surgeon general's vision for a healthy and fit nation.* Retrieved from http://www.surgeongeneral.gov/

Winokur, J. (1990). *Writers on writing.* Philadelphia: Running Press.

Wirt, W. (1836). Sketches of the life and character of Patrick Henry, as reproduced in L. Copeland & L. W. Lamm (Eds.), *The world's great speeches.* New York, Dover, 1973. Retrieved from http://www.history.org/almanack/life/politics/giveme.cfm

Index